Her We Serve

Her
We
Serve

Poems & Stories

Timothy P. McLaughlin
with a Foreword by David Abram

CULTURE CELEBRATING NATURE

Thunderous Press & Studios
Santa Fe, New Mexico
A subsidiary of Praising Earth, Inc., a New Mexico Nonprofit Corporation

Copyright © 2025 Timothy P. McLaughlin

All Rights Reserved.
This book may not be reproduced, in whole or in part, stored in a retrieval system, or transmitted in any form or by any means without permission from the publisher, except by a reviewer who may quote brief passages.

Cover Photograph: welcomia / ShutterStock.com
Cover and text design by Isla Kirkey

ISBN 979-8-9900930-2-7

PraisingEarth.org

ALSO BY THE AUTHOR

Rooted & Risen
Seeds Under the Tongue

IN MEMORY OF

JOHN JOSEPH MCLAUGHLIN III

1942–2023

CONTENTS

xiii   Foreword
       by David Abram

BONE
3   Subsumed
4   In the Forest
5   Animal Lines
7   Clawed and Fanged
9   Windswept
10   Taken and Given
12   Containers
14   Snowbanks
15   What Home Means

SKIN
19   In the Shadow of Deer
21   Painted
23   Heart Doctor
25   Claimed
26   Seeing in the Dark
27   Elsewise
29   Swimming in Beaver Tracks
32   Ten Men
34   Ballroom Dancing
36   Aflame
37   Mutiny
39   Another Chance

BREATH
43   Below
44   Asleep
45   Tending
46   Premonitions

48 Distractions
49 Galisteo Basin
52 Sindh
54 Murdering Trees
56 The Healers
58 Enough

BLOOD
63 How Gratitude Is
64 Currency
65 Family Lore
68 Girl Child
69 Backward
70 Scarring
72 Between Men
74 Mutilated
76 *In Cruce Glorior*
79 Reminders
80 Caesura
81 Pop
83 Hand to Hand
85 Falling

PULSE
89 Green Man
91 Forest for Us
94 Dirt on Our Hands
96 Elephants
99 Culture

102 Her We Serve
104 What It Is
107 Ma Says
110 Being Held

MYTH
113 New Queen, New Children
115 The Young Man and the Crone
120 The Well of Eloquence
125 The Boy, the Bear, and the Gold Ring
130 The King and the Deer Maiden
135 The Stranger

141 Acknowledgments

FOREWORD
by David Abram

How does a man of capacious heart and intelligence craft an honorable life in an era of civilizational collapse? Wandering among so many earthly wounds, how can he do honor to the radiant woman he deeply loves, and to the gifted children they raise together, while sustaining and sheltering them all? Yet more central, how can he fashion a life that blesses the living land around them – a life that steadily feeds the wild, half-broken, yet still exuberant earth to whose continued flourishing he has pledged his body, mind, and soul?

The poems and tales in this book form an incidental record of my friend Timothy P. McLaughlin's ongoing quest to carve such a full-round life. His quest cannot help but resonate with myriad young artists and parents and seekers in this uncanny era. The poetic sparks given off by his strivings carry clues and hints for those who seek to remain true to what matters.

McLaughlin often writes poems less for the page than for the tongue. Having lived, learned, and taught for three stormy years half a lifetime ago on a native reservation in South Dakota, he is now an oral, performance poet (as one cluster of rhyming lyrics, printed herein under the heading of *"Pulse"*, may make evident). This emphasis on spoken poetics follows from his craft as a ritualist, as one who is called upon by the community to guide seasonal ceremonies, solo fasts, and initiatory rites. McLaughlin is given to talking with cloudbursts and dragonflies and tall ponderosa pines.

He apprentices himself to free-flowing rivers, takes dictation from boulders, and is apt to burst into spontaneous bouts of praise for the enveloping mist, for a frog he spies in the shallows, for a snowshoe hare whose prints cross his path. He sometimes leads long dances, for men, that last multiple days and nights.

Whether he's whittling a teaching story for his son or an alchemical song for his daughters, whether he's tracking an antlered deer through the wooded mountains or tracking a sorrow that haunts the hidden depths of his own flesh, whether basking in a patch of glimmering moonlight, or burying himself among the writhing roots underground, McLaughlin is always working to heal humans back into the wider tangle of the land, to entwine the many-voiced eloquence of the forest with his human tongue. *"To be held, as the earth finally holds us, both earth and us thereby enlarged, is everything."*

"We are all praising, praying to
The light we are, but cannot know."

—WENDELL BERRY
Sabbath Poem, 1985 III

BONE

SUBSUMED

Perched on the forested steeps,
All that was adrift in me comes home.

Above, songbirds tone their
Early morning warmings.

Below, the stream gurgles and
Glides down to the village.

I become still. I sink in further.
Whatever is me dissolves.

The forest mind absorbs mine.
The valley fold is my bigger body.

If only I could remain thus.
I can however return here.

And knock upon the green door
Of the mountain. It always opens.

IN THE FOREST

Living among the scrub junipers
and pines that grow like bushes,
as much out as up, I often seek the
shelter of the mountain forests where
I can drift through the green village
of high stretched trunks given equally
to sky and soil. It's mostly silence
they offer me, as that is most needed.
Yet somewhere along the humus-padded
slopes, in the warming field of the
trees' everfresh perfumes and dappled
shadows, the voices I attend begin
their rich babble. Thus have I known
poetry. Thus have sticky fogs lifted
off my heart. Thus have I distinguished
callings from illusions. And more than
once have I stripped my feet bare
and dug my toes into the rocky black,
lifted my arms to the blue ceiling
and felt certain the big trees would
make me theirs, let me root in and
crust over and leaf out and tenderly
hold my sole place in the wild world.

ANIMAL LINES

Following the smooth single line
of what must be skunk's tracks in
the fresh snow, there is nothing
else. I sense how he slid under
and around fallen logs and low
brush, skipped over holes, avoided
snags. Skimmed along with enviable
grace and without missing a beat.
Quite unlike me, who crushes
heavy-footed prints into the
delicacy, my way blurred by
stumbles and slips, my rhythm
hiccupped by frequent snags and
stops. But, running his line, easing
into his swift-pawed prowess, being
led through the trees, this is bliss.
I can nearly see the dark-light
striped fur ahead, his thick tail
fanned out and lightly feathering
the snow. I am altogether there
behind him. Until my mind strays.

I instantly lose the trail and am
taken into another fold of pillowy
hillside. Here there are other tracks,
bigger, deeper, more intervaled.
A doe, I presume, and skirt the curls
of her bounding path. The way is
steep and exhilarating. After a
week of screen-rapt stasis, I am
ravenous for the heat of pumping
legs and beading sweat. Eventually,

I break from her trail as well and glide
down to the canyon bottom to sit in
the heaped glory of the year's first big
snow. A mighty pine, wet-laden with
the heavy blanketing, abruptly cracks
at its core and whirls in the wind,
groaning and leaning and finally
succumbing to a tremendous ripping
popping crash upon the earth.

As I scramble, head-covered, to a
higher perch, the sky is bulleted with
limbs and needles and rich-scented
with spewed sap. My tiny panting
organism is dumbstruck. The rooted
giants stand on in solemn witness
of winter's initial blow. However
it comes, may I too die and fall
with such thunder and such grace.

CLAWED AND FANGED

When I ramble far enough into the
wilds, a timidness sometimes stirs in
me, sensing I am the most anemic animal
around and the only who will depart

before dark to sleep indoors, away from
the swarming fungi. But then I run my
nails along my arm and my finger over
my teeth ridges and ponder if I've ever

really employed these primary tools.
Not merely to scratch off paint or rip
plastic but to claw up a tree in pursuit
or flight, or to bite something not already

dead. Just to know what it's like, as a boy
wonders how it feels to land an arrow in
an elk or be received inside a woman. And
I partly lament the cages of my comfortable

life, too often frozen before a glowing screen
whose barrage of dings and flashes are a
sinister sort of fangs into flesh. But when
the sun breaks through with its unguarded

beaming or the air is suddenly floated with
fat snowflakes twirling, that raw charm
unsmothers my heart. I stop worrying if
I will slip on the sheer ridge or how I

match up to the big eaters, and begin simply
moving through the landscape, my breath
huffing audibly, my feet nimbly negotiating
the loose steep terrain, my eyes finding the

faint tracks of paw paddings, my mind
mingling with that native ease. Then,
when I'm really in it, I hardly miss a step
or snap a twig; I lock into a sort of lithe

glide that defies the prescribed limits of
my middle-aged body. Enraptured, I've
forgotten the feebleness of my kind and
even the specifics of my own face, and

who's to say I haven't sprouted feathers
or fur, or pushed out claws and fangs,
and found my place, for an instant, in the
breathings and dreamings of wild ones.

WINDSWEPT

It's just a feeling, though it seems more.
In some sense, you're always seeking it.
It's the reason you wander blindly into
the unspoiled wilderness. It's why you drive
your legs for miles—over boulders and along
ridges, through thorns and mud, hungrily
tracking. But it's never where anyone says
it will be and won't come when called.
When your pluck slacks, it slips in and
sieges you. Abruptly, your mind is wiped
clean and your body is hijacked by a
wholesale intoxication that found you,
or was found, yet innocently, without tools
or strategy. Bewildered and bubbly, you
are buoyed into flight and coast through
the thick wet grasses, hoping to never find
your way out. For only the buzz and blur
of this unmoored storm can entirely unknot
the complex of cords that hold you fast in the
ruthless sobriety of reasonable living. Back in
the stuffed chair, you find yourself drawing up
reprises of that mesmerizing float where you
were intently, lucidly there, yet altogether gone.

TAKEN AND GIVEN

Meandering up a steep gully, I turn
into a narrow crook and come upon
a stunning rock face. Water spills
over its sheer jeweled brow and
mists into my dry nostrils. The clapping
song of stream upon stone penetrates
me like strong fingers kneading my
neck. My wandering halts; I am fixed
before this alluring architecture. In my
swoon, a voice floats from the mossed rock:

> *You flit about feverishly yet take ages to
> align with anything like purpose.*
>   *If you let one thought stretch over this valley,
> you'd do more than most moderns.*
>   *If you followed a single feeling to its end,
> you'd have more to say than the usual tellers.*
>   *If you pressed your entire heart against my
> stony chest, the medicine would surpass all healings.*
>
>   *Lean upon me for one day's twirl in space;*
> *Accompany me at least that far;*
>   *Feel the sun beat into your bones;*
> *Let the grime cake on your skin;*
>   *Stand firm as the wind whips in your ears;*
> *Upturn your face to the lashing rain.*

*Remain planted beside me, and I will show
you a little of how I eat sunlight,
     how I drink star glow. All night I will pour
a stream of stone lore into your mouth.
     I will loan you my seat in the big dreaming.
Then when you uproot from here and go on
     buzzing in and out of everyplace, as befits you,
you will carry an inkling of what it is
     to stay put, to know your rightful place,
and do your only work.*

CONTAINERS

I walk far into the bosom of
    a sweetwater
mountain where even the echoes

of inner sneering monsters have
    resolved into wind
whisper. Held together too long

by duty, I swiftly unravel under
    cloak of trees.
Clobbered by freed grief, I drop

in a heaving heap till my dark
    tears run clear
again. I've come to the end of

the line I toed and resented.
    Will I vanish
completely? If I shrug off my

torments here, what load will
    occupy these
restless arms? I am strangely

weightless, lifted, uncontained.
    My body is
floated up the ridgeline. My feet

are apace yet I deploy no muscle.
    My hands present
but the flesh is hardened, coarse,

ancient. My throat gurgles out
    an arrhythmic chant,
more underwater slip-speech than

language. I've slid into some other
    sequence altogether.
Nothing is as it was. I can hear

but cannot tell if the soundings
    are within or
without. I'm not sure what my

name is now or which of this is
    or isn't me.
I am here but dissolved away.

It seems I could go on a long
    while this way.
The mountain is bottomless.

SNOWBANKS

In the high mountains,
The winter snowbanks seem
Immovable.

Yet sunshine slowly sinks
Their walls until,
Wondrously,
Clear water gushes forth.

So too there were stores
Of treasure bound in me
Freed by years
Of your penetrating smile.

Sometimes we are
The catchers and sometimes
The releasers.

And sometimes, for a long
While, the snow refuses to fall.
Or the sun hides away
In gray clouds.

So we wait. And remember.
And just when we've accepted their
Final disappearance,

The flakes twirl down to pile
In great heaps.
And the light flickers and strobes
Through the haze.

WHAT HOME MEANS

Climb the hills until you reach
the source waters of the place you belong.
Make love with the mountain there,
you and the spring upwelling together,
goodness streaming into the valleys
and lesser slopes. Feel the stretch of the
water's region, held now in your eye
and, forevermore, your breast. Go too
to the place the river conjoins with the
greater waterway, looking back, recalling
the high green spot, the stony peak, the view.
If you can access it, trek your way to the
center between origin and confluence
and stand still, inscribing your heart in
the outlying spheres, those below of clay
and stone and those above of star and cloud.
Without this, you are nowhere and will
fall to pieces upon the slightest pressure.
With this, you are given and then known—
dust as much your breath as sky,
minerals sweatily co-mingled with your cells,
the humus beneath a fluid extension
of your feet. Then you will know what
it is to merge with a mountain spring.
And nothing less will satisfy.

SKIN

IN THE SHADOW OF DEER

I gave up my ruined culture when it
said, Choose: feed your belly or
your soul. I fled to the Dakota prairie
and was given a temporary seat on
the fringes of a native culture, its
core unbroken despite a century of
ravagement. After three winters there,
changed, I returned to the Virginia
woods of my youth where a short-antlered
buck recognized my transfiguration
and gave me something I yet carry,
and more so carries me. There I bound
myself to buck beyond my knowing,
like a newly potent boy firing seed into
a hazy future. Nearly three decades later,
I often find deer scat and prints and
change my course to his, a worthy lead
whose trots and bounds uncage me
from myself. Now my life is further
bound to a storied desert basin that
looks forever east. At three key points
in this watershed, a gleam of bony white
caught my eye and breath. Three times
I knelt with a palmful of tobacco. Three
antlers I scooped into my clutch. And
three-fold is the medicine the deer gifted
me. Attuned to this, an elder woman
one day laid a spotted hide upon my back
and the shell of well-mannered man
crumbled to release a wilder being. Now

I, like deer, am hunted and must tuck myself into the shadows of a world gone mad. At times, I wish to starve or leap into the mighty gorge—what place is there for me and mine? Yet a flickering light keeps on within, kindled by the old myths I heard and tell. At the right moment, with the right archer, I will unveil my long horns and white-furred chest and let the arrow pierce my heart. It is as the deer have always done.

PAINTED
for Basil Brave Heart

When we emerged from the willow lodge, he
painted lines beneath my eyes and called me
a warrior. Simply because I had stayed three
years in his remote native village, held on

through crushing crises and howling winters,
and lingered long enough to witness the unspeakable
and impossible (humans and thunders in other-
worldly dialogue) and never backed away.

Just that, the staying with, meant so much
to a man formed of the light clay of reservation
lands, whose heart secrets away each night
to the nearby Black Hills where his ancestors

invisibly circulate. In classic Lakota generosity,
he painted me, then told me that when I leave
all I really need to pray is a cup of water. And a
bit of lit sage. Water. And fire. Fire and water.

Nodding, I didn't greatly understand what I was
told by such humble oracle. Twenty-five years hence,
I now live by the mysterious governance of those
two, the water and the fire. What they say, how

they ripple and swirl, the smoke and the bubbles,
the churning, the stillness, the searing off of
dead thought, the billowy inflow of new guidance,
the wrinkles and cracks of things that last.

Each time I lay an altar to sit with these
elementals, the flame speaks afresh, the pool
weirdly absorbs and mirrors. Something is
revealed. And, when I receive a person who sat

upon the mountain some days and nights, I
likewise present these two to them, fire and
water fresh-painted below their eyes, a map of
belonging already inscribed beneath the tough

skin formed in learning over and over how to hide
away in plain sight. The firelight unveils us again.
The springs restore our moist nature. In that
homecoming, we can each stand and be painted.

HEART DOCTOR

When the first half of my life ended, I chopped
my hair at the chin. The long curls whispered
down and piled in a clump that looked poised
to walk off as its own animal, hungry as any.
Hawk smelled the wound of shorn hair and
came circling, in curiosity or opportunity.
For many days, he kept finding me or waiting
somewhere to be found, like a trusted friend.
And he'd open those huge spotted arms and
bare his chest to me, then circle and circle until
I couldn't help but entreat him to eat out the dead
parts of my dogged heart. So broken was I by
the grim world, this was the only conversation
I could manage, to unbutton my shirt and be
pecked at until the poison was mostly gone
and I could again brave the company of another
human. The day I lit a fire and the smoke of my
smoldering hair streamed over the trees, hawk
dove into view for the last of his visits. He snared
me in his fixed gaze then spun me around as if
I were puppet-strung to his maneuvers: my arms
outstretched like his, my legs back-pedaling and
head wobbling backward to keep him in sight.
He rose like a geyser, dipping in and out of
blaring sunlight until the dot of him disappeared
altogether and I flopped to the dirt, cords-cut.
Blinded and shaken, I lifted the top half of me
from the earth. There was a soothing and a
warming in my chest. And words simmering.
Or perhaps a tune, wordless and airy, erupting

first as just a chuckle, then filling out in roars and sighs. When it silenced, I stood full mast and felt new guidance return about which way to walk. And I could feel my hair growing back.

CLAIMED

When they come for you, it's
never in error. Some curve of
bone, some dab of color, some
slight gesture marks you as
theirs and they descend in
flashes and rumbles to claim
you. Though nothing is more
dangerous, the rightness volts
you forward into that electrified
ring of belonging. In one blow,
they slash your cheek and scalp
your sickly mind, then hurl you
into the dying camps to do what
only you can, fingertips stained
ice-blue and eyes blurred with
water. More and more, you are
given to the dreaming and have
no more place in the sunlight
and little time for the day to
day. When your hand fills with
heat, things happen that you must
answer to. Understood or not,
you won't be alone again.
You belong to the thunders.

SEEING IN THE DARK

As much as I prize you, oh sun, these days
it's lesser lit images that bewitch my heart:
a ring of men thumping drums on a mesa
top, the bearded face beside me and the
waxing moon above both aglow in fire
flicker; moving in pace with the shadowy
body curving in bed beneath me, upon
me, before me, lengthening and coiling
like a slick jellyfish adrift; standing blanket-
wrapped all night in a stone circle, the
impenetrable black slowly brightening
into morning's ceremonious unfurl. My
eyes hanker for these. Who dares flip on
a hissing bulb when the house begins to
brim with luscious darkness? What
shut-eyed rest compares with the soothe
of each thing going invisible in the prelude
of a readying dream? Enfolded in night's
pitch, I am of everything, so what could
I fear? And what could fear me who gazes
out blindly into the scene that broadens
and broadens until nothing is there, save
a quiet lapping upon an unseen shore?

ELSEWISE

Who called me to this meeting?
Why are there no throbbing drums here to warm us?
How can I listen when there is no storyteller?

If this balderdash is called speaking, what hand
Lodged such dead language in us?
Can my tongue be unlearned?
What spirit would quicken to make me its mouthpiece?

What is this blind trap sold to me as life?
When did my gray brain begin believing it was
Other than earth clay?
How did my pink heart forget its pumping
Sources the bubbling springs?

If I secret myself away from this circus,
Who will miss me?
What magnificent beasts, supposed extinct,
Await my escape and sham extinction?

How do my naked feet know this thin track
Through the fearsome forest?
Why do I smell a wetness in the dark trees?
If the forest swallows me, will I surface some
Otherwhere with a new face?

Where is the real king?
When will he take me to the wild witch already
Spinning the story to carry us out?
The story that dreams me down to meet it.

For there is an elsewhere silently forming and
An elsewise softly rising.
Underneath all this hardness.

SWIMMING IN BEAVER TRACKS

At the men's camp,
I break from the group to
consort alone with the river.

Scrambling down the steep
crumble of Chama River Canyon,
the land underfoot is thickly

decorated with colored stones.
My eye is caught over and over
by whites and purples popping,

by swirls and stripes imprinted,
yet the surging river beckons, insists.
I go to where I saw beaver

swim this early morning, gliding
along the brown surface,
submerging and reemerging

in sleek aquatic knowing.
Reaching the shoreline, I strip
down to skin and hair

and step toward the waters.
I'm instantly engulfed to the knee
by covetous mud and sinking

quickly. I yank one leg free and
plunge for the bank, clawing
my naked form from the

wet depths: humbled, experienced.
But not unraptured. I track the
river edge for stonier ground

and mark a choice spot
upstream. I scoop my garments
and set off, hiking barefoot

and bare-bodied, my unsheathed
paws finding superior holds
on uneven rocks and loose soil.

Does beaver see me?
Is my attempt toward wildness
amusing? Does my exuberance

attract or divert her? Can she
scent the tobacco I sprinkled
for her? Spot the wildflowers

I laid out in her name?
At last, I plunge my heated
organism into the icy water.

The silty current rushes over
my outstretched body.
Toes anchored in slick stones,

arms reaching ahead, I have
taken flight in this roaring
paradise. The sky goes gray

above me. A storm looms.
Re-clothed, I clamber back upward.
The camp is waiting. A young brother

is setting the sacred fire. An elder man
waddles down the path to his
place in the circle. I carry a stone

in my hand and a story in my eyes.
The rain beads on my bare chest
and mixes with lingering silt,

recoloring me. Tonight, we will
dance by firelight and moon glow.
When I saunter weightless through

the sagebrush to my tent among soft
flashes of lightning, I will say I
have really lived at least one day.

TEN MEN

If you were there when ten men sat circled
around the red sparking fire, themselves encircled
by a ring of stout redwoods all bottom-charred
from the prowling licks of earlier fires; if you

heard them, contrary to all training, abandon
the comforts of polite speech and daringly address
the fire as the old god it is, shucking layers of
hardened heart armor they'd sleepily strapped on

year after year, and one-by-one coming to a
kind of clarified language almost alien in its
tender tones and breathy phrases (one man
somewhere between song and speech, reshaping

his heart matter in the steady hold of the gang);
if you were there as the cedar warmed in their
palms while they spoke, then was thrown to the
flames like long-held seeds suddenly spewed

into the hot well of earth, making the glowing
coals sizzle and coo at the surge of leaf stuff
landed; if you too were among them when they
discovered something only knowable by pressing

and pressing their naked feet against the cool earth
in the wild dancing that overtook them; if you had sat
with them that late summer day in the tree-dappled
light and felt your own mouth open in a new shape

and your body buzz in a fresh beholding (like hungry
lovers anticipating, like fervent lovers engaged)
could you ever leave that forest for the city's narrow
corridors and conversings? Or rather would the forest,

the fire, the cracking cedar, the blood thrumming
in ten men's chests ever leave you, no matter how long
you waited to again watch the flame wind up through
the sticks and wink away your every resistance?

BALLROOM DANCING

I've come down from the mountain and entered
the big room where everyone is named brother.
I've dipped my toes into a little-known river

of belonging. There's a pulsing even before the
drums begin. In their thunder, a delicious madness
claims us, three hundred men rising from the stiff

chairs of this windowless place to band in the
center and pound the smooth-tanned hides, the walls
melting around us as we drive a desperate plea

for something more on and on into the big
Mystery who looms with a mouth full of questions:

What is this song you're thumping out?
Why did you go drumless and silently yearning for so long?
Is your heart likewise awake again and wet with rhythm?
Will you feed it to the river left unfed for ages?

There's heat and water in my eyes now. The
dazzling desert autumn has crushed into the room
and these men have all turned to cottonwoods

who cannot hide the gold beaming on their
boughs or muffle the leaf song clattering
in their throats. The hard ballroom floor beneath

us fissures in a maze of lightning lines. Tiny
tendrils sprout from our unclothed feet and
wriggle down in the rooting we were made for.

And then we begin to *dance*: like rooty trees,
like wondrous beasts. Remembering ourselves
anew, a Babelic mish-mash of speaking bodies

erupts in the wild dancing discourse we'd waited
our lives to find. A finding you could scour continents
to seek and never reach. A finding that noiselessly

waits in the plainest stand of trees or gentlest
floating river, that presents itself in the anyplace
where you stand wholly stripped and feel a

drumming in the dark clay, or catch a gleaming on
the water, and reach out to push open the doorway
where the known softly gives way to the real.

AFLAME

Beware those whose immediate affection
runs too hot
Praise that is lavish and relentless will
surely burn out
Trust more the bonds that build with
with ease
Electric connection followed by
space and stillness
Storm waters pounding down, drunk
in over time
Yet we are fiery and forgetful and love
to fall in love
Though we know the danger, we will still
be scalded sometimes
May we forgive our lovers for overstocking
the fire
When we find the right heat
we are free
To let our care for everyone run
on and on
Like a clear mountain stream that cannot
stop giving

MUTINY

They drank from our cups.
They sat at our fireplaces.
They bedded in our chambers.
And gladly.

We opened, and opened more.

They longed to walk in starlight.
They gripped our pantlegs
To steady them in the dark.

They lusted for the depths.
They pulled the air from our lungs
To sustain them underwater.

They begged for a key to the house.
And left it in shambles.

They ate the fruits
But never watered the vines.

We are left washing soiled walls.
We are left collecting dead seeds.

We have been here before.

They are nameless
And countless. And blind
To their crimes.

More like them will come.
But we are wiser.

And the magic given us runs deep.

All will be replenished.
They know not the source.
Nor the sourcing.

ANOTHER CHANCE

The world was silenced
To make me finally listen.
My ears long pummeled
By the facile mantras
Of modernity, it all
Suddenly hushed. A
Relentless deafness
Engulfs me, unmoors
Me. Even asleep, I am
Spinning. Lost in the
wilds of my bruised mind.
I am brought to the edge
Where being incarnate
Presents as a choice.
I turn inward.
I apprentice myself to
Silence. I conjure an
Animal know-how.
Hunting, I am however
Caught in the jaws of a
Greater beast. Eaten, I
Merge with its blood.
Digested, what was me is
Obliterated. Dead and
Dumped, I am food again.
Only then can I enter the
Seed of my next self. Only
Then are all traces of
Illness expunged.
Traversing great mother's
Soil canals, I am her
Initiate. She breathes me

Back into the very body
That was deafened.
Hearing much more.
Hearing everything.
All my old lives are
Stacked behind me. This
Time, I've got the trick
Of things. I find myself
Speaking. These words
Belong to no one. They
Pass through, cloud-like.
Wet the imagination, and
Move along. All things
Possible, I choose to sit
Forever by a mountain
Stream. The glisten and
Gush are untiring. As is
My rapture. Even just
To breathe is astonishing.
Surely I'll die again
Before I'm through.

BREATH

BELOW

I am concerned with the subtle workings
    of roots elaborately jumbled underground;

wound together like secret lovers under cover
    of dark, where nothing is plainly beheld but

felt in a deep-down, unspoken way. My lusty
    heart quickens at the puzzlement of below,

of the unseen, of that which breaks into the
    apparent and the upright risen form. I thirst

for the tremor of moist black soil sparking
    an underneath circuitry, a soft pulsing within

this earth that gives movement
    to each above thing. That is where my mind

travels in the still of night. When I have
    vanished, be sure I am there, among the roots.

ASLEEP

Why do the masters make so
much of being awake when I
find the work happening more
and more in sleep, sequence
after dense sequence of dream
colliding in a drive that chips
away at the big waking inertia
that cannot abide the light-
quick pace of the cosmos? My
stiff daytime uprightness shears
away too much of the rich
fiber of worlds which present
at night, in the warm shut-eyed
collapse where I see far more
than the light reveals. Let me
stay asleep, tunneling farther
and farther into that aroused
reality which strives toward
nothing but surpasses all
pretenses of clarity in one
instant of its dazzled imagery.
My sleeping body roils all
night in the wild surf of a
thunderbolt's gleaming innards,
tossed about in that yellow
glare, stupefied by an intelligence
unknown to any waking mind.

TENDING

How easily any one of us
Contemplates the rifle or the rope,
Sensing no direction but out—
Of the body, of the earth,
Of the overwhelm in merely
Surviving. And how mercifully
Does the pained heart release
In the wash of cello strings or
A kind word landed just so.
The tower of hurt topples
Momentarily. It rebuilds itself
Of course. Yet to rest, even
Three heartbeats, in the gaze
Of one who has become clear,
Who looks without grasping,
Is high rare medicine.
In the worst terror, in the
Death throes, the trees never
Stop tending each other.
Humanity too is a sort of
Forest. Love is sunlight
And acceptance is water.
Sunny or rainy, we are fed
And we feed.

PREMONITIONS

How often do we know what's real
but clutter the ground with splinters
of what isn't? How plainly truth
speaks in us, our neck squeezed tight
against a poorly fitting invitation,
our lungs relaxed in the heat of the
next apt gateway glimpsed. When
tasked the wrong work, our hands
tellingly falter. And when we finally
lift the hammer to the grey dam that
quells all our innate premonitions,
our forehead rings with yes, yes, god
yes. Is it so too with our final going
forth? What is in the field days before
a big water blasts in to claim legions
of us? What is felt as the fire and terror
of war begins its sickish simmer
toward bloody overboil? Maybe,
being earth's infants, we are kept
innocent of the hard news piped along
lines of fungi, scooped by the leafed
and shouldered by the antlered who
soberly ready the grounds for inevitable
flames or floods. Still, if departing,
when do we sense ourselves begin to
spirit up like smoke or seep down like
groundwater? Is there more to know
than we bear to acknowledge? What is
this acceleration jittering our hearts
now? This overwhelm of insight

that demands some strange conversion,
like a fresh skin given, made of feathers
or star dust, feeling at first foreign
but somehow, increasingly, just right.

DISTRACTIONS

In a world built of distractions, how do we sober enough to regard the earth unflinchingly, to permit the anguish pounding in the soil to pound likewise in us, to face the crushing imprint of all we've ravaged and left bereft? In the middle of that brutality, might a slight wind rise to bolster our labored breath or a spear of light appear that punctures the prevailing fog? Something to assure us the lasting treasures of this blue orb are yet kept sound, the foremost truths safely secreted away under cover of the ever more cunning web of distractions.

GALISTEO BASIN

Red dirt, red boulders,
A litter of pottery shards.
Soft sink of foot, an open
View: mountain spikes,
River coils, cactus poise
And cedar sprawl. Stone
Etchings catch the breath,
Echo the ancient eros of
Hunter and hunted.
Gridwork gardens and
Half-buried walls recall
An ancient people in
Prosperity. A nearer
Flicker of shepherd
Prints, of grazing fields,
And stacked stone ruins.
Nearer still are the
Heavy leavings of miners'
Lust, upturned black earth,
Flash of gold-drunk grins.
A no-knowledge time:
Crash of sawed pines,
Choke and smear, rough
Trappings and skinnings,
Dead animals and murky
Waters, the railway's
Endless probe. Then:
A quieting, a burrowing
Down, lonely whisky sip
And hazy gun barrel rub.

The upspring of surveyors'
Pointy lines, chop and
Grab, infestation of wires
And locks, cow tromp and
Chew, no right to roam.
Now: The land sits (private
Or protected, abused or
Neglected) awaiting its
Limp-hearted lover. An
Ember hums in the dead
Coals, the green world
Beckons. The sapient
Remembers itself as
Five-fingered *animal*, ignoble
Yet tender, tenacious,
Real. Fists exhaust their
Hold, taking gives way
To tending. Abuser and
Worshipper alike wisp
To ash. A queer return
To mud hut and drum
Strike, the unlikely
Resurrect of picked
Medicines and wild-grown
Foods, of thunder talk
And water catch, of stories
Scratched in dirt and
Songs hummed on
Waterways. The strange
Upright beast is refaced,

Wielding a basic parlance
Of praise, acting nine
Generations forward, gently
Belonging and intently
Longing for fresh passages
In the dark mythology
Of a silty riverside place.

SINDH

If you can, you must go there. The Indus River Valley.

The smoothest way into that fortressed desert kingdom is to slip through a crack in the old, low-built mud walls that extend beyond the reaches of today's well-policed, high wire fences.

Inside, the sand shimmers, the river meanders, the wine flows, and the singer's voice resounds to coax the clouds down to shade that sun-blistered place apart.

Wielding the plain-speak of commerce, you will receive only polite grins. Bearing the hardened heart of a general, you will mistake exuberance for hot-bloodedness, invitation for danger.

Entering rather with your hands and pockets empty and gazing with the astonished eyes of a poet, you will know Sindh for who she is: a fertile river valley fed generously by rich folklore rising

from the teller's hands as he animates the tent lit by oil lamps with his rollicking, rhythmic intonations. And you will feel the solidity of a people who hold a common heart pumped through

with the everfresh verses of their favored poets who once walked those vast deserts, wild-eyed and open-hearted, carrying only a stringed instrument and a tongue on fire for the Beloved.

Bound to truth, they sang—in village or forest, among the people or with the birds—until the poems stretched on and on, like the river, spilling into the sea and fastening a people together with the

unbreaking ease of liquid. Over centuries, that language has been
braided into the very soil and seeps up into the unsuspecting foot soles
of its sons and daughters and rattles their ribs until the lines are spoken

aloud again, sung into the air where they dance like whirling bees,
fat-bellied with honey that drips from the few trees left standing in this
kingdom that now lives only in the glowing eyes of those Sindhis who

remember, who cannot forget, who hold the true Sindh within them.

MURDERING TREES

When a man, Boniface, later named a saint,
ordered the thick-armed woodcutters to fell
an ancient tree long regarded as sacred, do
you think demons streamed from the exposed
trunk as he suspected? Or did that great woody
elder bleed widely into the ground where
it had stood for generations as a doorway to
the upper and the lower, as something to be
trusted beyond any human or nation, and a thing
no human or nation, in any dark fit, would harm?
And when this future saint watched the giant
thunder oak crash and found himself ostensibly
unscathed (only because nature, in its extravagant
mercy, didn't strike him down in return),
his lust for seeking apparent demons and
condemning them rose like an insatiable beast.

So it went with other trees that might otherwise
still be anchored in soil, holding the deeper reality
together. Instead the stumps and dry roots now
attract only unseen congregations of ancestors,
those who stood by on the fateful chopping days
and felt the first axe blow as if it were delivered to
their own chests, and bellowed out in keens that the
ashamed woodsmen and all who knew the Goddess
heard plainly and were troubled by thereafter.

All was changed. Earth now served humanity and
men bowed only to an above-earthly God. Gifts
were left less and less at holy springs and revered
peaks and only under cloak of night. If a word
of thanks was breathed for any natural marvel

(staggering rainbows, tracts of wildflowers) or gift (deer hunted, rye risen), it was offered not directly to the beauty or the harvest but to the one who ruled earth from afar. This distance has made all the difference. Even today we feel ourselves apart and can't quite make out the waves roiled with plastic, can't exactly feel the mountain violated repeatedly by machinery, or the animals laying down sick and starved, or the fresh-sapped trees toppling in the now unspoken creed of our species: Do as we please and never pay the bill.

Will the saints and martyrs bring us fresh water when we've run out? Can their miracle-apt hands turn back the rising heat? Or shall we, like them, at the sight of flames advancing, just press our palms together, fingertips pointed up to the heaven that awaits at least the best of us? If this pale blue ship is sinking into the deep black, I prefer to go down with it, falling like a massive oak, tumbling through the vastness: uprooted, disowned, unpurposed, becoming again...

THE HEALERS

They stand huddled in white
    coats, squinting at charts

and throttling figures in a
    desperate crusade for

certainty. They scrutinize blood
    and food and the cosmos, and

record everything, sensing
    they are coming closer.

I speak of a farmer's breath
    feeding the field, a grandma's

tears dissolving a lump—
    the invisible and incalculable.

They grip and rattle their
    skulls feverishly, then break up

in roaring laughter. They hold
    the blade, the syringe before

me and say they'd insert it
    unblinkingly in their own

child. They insist every inch
    of earth be examined, inside

and out. They assemble all
    the findings and will live or

die by the computations.
    When shaken to the core, though,

half of them can be found
    knelt in a stuffy block house

intoning supplications to the
    image of a man said to be

born from no sperm.
    The other half stay home,

probing and probing
    the unwieldy darkness,

demanding to know
    what its real plans are.

I've seen a bare-chested old
    man pour water over heated

stones and gently ask the
    steam to soften a stuckness.

Because they knew him—
    the stones, the water—

and because his heart opened
    for the person sitting before him,

the medicine was administered.
    In immeasurable doses.

ENOUGH

Enough. Is enough.
Yet we refuse to
curb our endless
lust for on and on
and more and more,
our swollen hubris
and skewed vision
and labyrinthine lives
shadowing the real.
Is there not yet an
unglorified animal
within who needn't
do more than walk
and gather and tend
and love and dream?
Who needn't do less
either. Who does not
diminish any piece of
life's web without
repaying it somewhere.
Who isn't quite noble
in this exchange, just
aware. Who is clear
of vision, light of foot,
deft of hand, flesh-
bound to fire, blood-
thread to water.
Breathing with the
mind of the forest.
Tracking the burn
of stars. Freed from
the compulsion to

know and tumbled
into the prospects
of unknowing. Wild
once more. Robust
again. Mossing out
like wet trees, feet
awash in rising
aquifers. Thickening
to fullness like thunder
clouds adrift in fresh
skies. Dreaming like
any creature whose
belly is full enough
to be happy and
empty enough to
hunger for life.

BLOOD

HOW GRATITUDE IS

The river of gratitude is so vast,
All streams absorb into it.

When you have chosen a habit
Of thanks,
Each thing gives way in time
To that enveloping current.
Even the terrors that gut you
Are wound up and carried along.

Sometimes it dives down
And goes underground
To protect itself
And flows on unseen,
Its inclusivity unmarred.

Even then there is little time
For your sharp complaints
Or fuzzy boredoms.
Every inch of the waterway
Awaits your praise.

And you have but one mouth
And two hands.
Yet the waves of allurement
Proceed into one another
Endlessly.

CURRENCY

Underneath the network of money we know,
there is a secret currency in motion.
One scrape of the fingernail at an edge
of murky air will peel back the coverings
that cloak this otherworldly reciprocity.

Consider: the same hour my wife slipped on
wet tile in a faraway temple and slammed
down upon her elbow, I stumbled into a shelf
at our home, sending an old pottery airborne
to smash to pieces. A Pueblo grandma told me
the pot took the blow for my darling's arm.

Or this: The very moment my yet unswimming
son lost his footing in a rushing river,
my gold marriage band was thrust from
my finger and flung downstream to live
among the drowned pebbles. *We took that
instead of him* rang in my dripping ears.

You have your tales also, grand or humble,
of this extraordinary give and take. Its maneuvers
override our careful bookkeeping and upset our
belabored predictions. Exchanges are made in
flashes our eyes are mostly unable for. Figures
move our hands in strokes only hazily recalled.

We took the pottery shards up the mountain
and buried them, a gifting back of clay to clay.
I spoke a blessing upon the ring now riverbound
(gold to feed the waters), and remarried my beloved:
ringless, a blanket enfolding our two given bodies.

FAMILY LORE

It's a story I love to tell. While in utero,
each of our three children oversaw
construction of a structure, a space to

match the dream being written in them.
The eldest, a stepdaughter for me, was
in the womb while a house was raised

and stuccoed upon the rocky perch we call
home that sits between three mountains.
A home and a dad, a lover for her mom;

mightn't one say her starry eyes becoming
sought these out from the dark belly waters?
When we assembled as a family, as unlikely

as any, a boy child soon pointed his staff
down through shafts of moonlight to stir
my hands into the builder's way. And day

after day, as he grew into himself and my
beloved's torso rounded, I mixed and
slapped mud together to make a hut where

he could emerge in the secret of night,
a round unmodern place where we began,
with his coming, the earth ceremonies

that anchor us yet, and likely always will.
And there were two who never came, never
called us to draw up sketches or lay down bricks

but just blinked in and out of body, throttling
our hearts with the only pain equal to the rapture
of catching a live child bawling with new breath.

That more than double sorrow led us to look
toward other sorts of building, but nothing came
of it. For years anything we grasped just

flaked to dust in our fingers and our sights
were accordingly narrowed, and then downcast.
Until a mythic string of summer nights when the

woman I adore danced under the stars with
twelve others, mothers and maidens alike,
beheld by four crones, until she became a leaping,

chanting, unruly, broadened being who would
bear life once more. And the third babe whispered
for the simplest yet strongest shelter of all:

a prayer lodge made of river willows
enclosed with blankets and tarps where
we can all be enwombed many times over.

These three containers hold us well, especially
while adventuring the ephemeral wild kingdom
called childhood that allows me entry

each day, once the board discussion quiets
and the computers blink off. And I pray all three
now home with me will one day discover

the more lasting comforts of the greatest earthly
shelters—rugged mountains—vast seas—
clouded skies—that turn black each night

and recall whatever clear callings we sounded
into the stars when we were first shaped as
peculiar, bodied, homebound, storytelling things.

GIRL CHILD

The year of her birth, I painted all the outer
doors of our home turquoise so the wild deer
who gave her to us would know where to find her.
And so no matter what she found in the circus
of the world, all her homecomings would be
dabbed with an insistent shininess. The blue
of her eyes is darker, sea-like, less bouncing the
light than pulling it in, holding a center that
transfixes whoever's caught in her gaze. Just a
year, milk yet dribbling from her chin, she's not
woman, not fully gendered as such, but surely
a female becoming and thus I marvel at each
new growth or sound, certain I will miss
the moment the witch-goddess arrives to fix
the feminine seed pod in her. When it splits and
sprouts its thousand curling tendrils, I'll admire
them from afar, silenced by their scintillations.
No doubt it will be my male heart she'll break
first when one day she turns and smiles in
the threshold, her long thin form framed in
smudged turquoise, stepping out with a purpose
I find mystifying. Such are the riches of a father's
secret coffer, to be unlatched at some dark time
when time no longer means much, the coins
clenched by the remnants of my once trusty grip
and walked into the shadowed wood where they
can be laid on the moist soil and swallowed
into the system of gifting that brings all children
to us gratis out of nothing and from nowhere.

BACKWARD

You came here, son, with wires crisscrossed in
the telltale pattern of storm clouds.

One fateful day, your eye began turning to the
strange pull of black and white strings.

Who schooled you in the ways of clowning?
And who is to accompany you backward through life?

Yet, why not contradict everything the foolhardy
human speaks?

Why not skip upstream along our vacuous
bobbing heads?

If you are here to freeze the things we thought
to melt, to unearth what we kept buried,

to loose the knots we fearfully wrenched,
to place an unwavering hand in the

fire's searing center, and to laugh and laugh
and laugh as the skies darken

and unleash the big rain written in your shrewd
grin and sideways gaze,

I will stand by steadfast, father to your odd body
and friend to your wily soul.

SCARRING

When you came to me, forearm self-split
spouting blood, eyes frenzied, and the
scream of *I'm so sorry Dad* in your trembling
throat, I wondered where and when we
had lost you. Baby sister clenched to my
side and little brother stood by wide-eyed
as I wrapped you tight and held on till
the gash clotted and we could breathe
again. The shadowy places lure us all in
at times and no father can stand guard at
every rabbit hole, but some tunnels twist
you past the point of return. And you were
halfway gone down perilous caverns before
we sniffed it out and snatched you back, your
innocence limp in your hands like a sorceress'
wand uncharmed. Yet your eyes were
unchanged, the same that peered up at me
at three to say *You're gonna marry my Mom*,
the same that glimpse only shadows of the
man whose face mirrors yours but who hasn't
come around to father you. One thing's certain:
no neat-knit rope could wrangle your story
in its rowdy turnings. Like your running
blood that day, your singing voice (wow,
wow) bursts out with irrepressible vigor.
And carries nuances beyond your years that
touch people far below the ordinary. I know
you will keep on, shining girl, fueled by an
enduring drive breathed in while you slumber
and traverse dreamlands. No guide accompanies
you there, and, upon waking, you and I must be
reintroduced and find our way again. And so

we do. And will. Each morning. Even when
you're grown. For our blood is now mixed
as one thick liquid we two carry everywhere.

BETWEEN MEN

One day you will come face to face with
A woman whose countenance echoes yours
And whose heart is scarred with the tracks
Of your flight; for reasons unknown, you left
Her adrift to seek alone the necessary steadying
That comes unbidden from the blood father.
So, she had to grow stronger quicker than
Your other three daughters. The ferocity in her
Eyes will quiver your knees as she stands
Unwavering, silent in the reckoning so long
Coming, in the name of her mother, my queen,
Who you loved and dropped. Yet the child of
Your seed remained. You will wonder at this
Gleaming girl now woman and at time passed,
Recalling who you were when she arrived and
How much has changed. Her fixed gaze will
Choke you in everything you can no longer
Say, for you missed the moment, all of them
Actually, and must abide the silence. It will be
Long past time for apologies. Rather, she will,
With the unequivocal grace of a woman, love
You anyway, break the false spell and allow you
To weep for all that was lost, in your boy's heart
And in the magnificent hearts of your and her
Taos ancestors who endured the violent trauma
That separated your people and who would never
Deny you and her this coming together. They
Will smile as the mildewed walls between father
And daughter momentarily crumble. There will be
Years of repair ahead, maybe more than you have
Left. And whether you ever shake my hand, I held
The tension these many years, stood as father for

One whose blood differs yet whose soul chose mine
As I chose hers, clearing the heaped wreckage
To open a new curve on the ever-greening path.
She weathered the absence of you with a dignity
Not to be expected of anyone. Time and again,
I have witnessed her rise after a night blanket-
Wrapped on the frozen soil, lift her face to the
Sunrise and sing her prayer to the surrounding
Stars. And I have adored her. Will you, too?

MUTILATED

On the second day of your life,
While you are still partway in the
Dream of warm watery bliss and
The feel of bright light and cold air
Is just settling in you, we will pry
You from the soft milky breast and
Whisk you into a room apart, pin you
Down on the hard table and violate
You with our sterile instruments—
Pulling and squeezing and snipping
Until your most sacred secret part
Is laid bare, raw and bleeding,
Then smothered with bandages. And
We will feel relieved. We will leave
You to sulk your way through this
First wounding. We will say you didn't
Really register the pain. We will say
The wailing is normal. And we will
Say: now you are one of us. And when,
If ever, you again feel entirely safe
In your nakedness, when another
Bare-skinned human has taken you in
So deeply that a dull aching rises from
Your always-exposed tip, we will name
It delusion. We will never connect
Patterns of aggression or waves of
Worthlessness to this routine procedure.
We will deny the crushing imprint of
Our heartless precautions. And, above
All, we will go on fearing nature. So
Fearful indeed that we will repeatedly
Take its most precious gifts into closed

Rooms and punish them beyond belief.
So they too will swallow the fear down
Whole and stay in line, head down, heart
Closed, the anguish of that primary
Unnatural act burning faintly thereafter.

IN CRUCE GLORIOR

Just pubescent but not yet stretched
To the six feet of muscled limbs that
Now carries me through many of life's
Scrapes, I crossed the Potomac River
From Virginia to the blaring center of
Washington DC where I was dropped
Wide-eyed into a prep school blur of
Outer privilege and dark understory
That would clobber my childhood to
Submission. Two weeks into it, my
Shiny purple bag bearing the Latinate
Crest of this prestigious academy (*In
Cruce Glorior*—Glory in the Cross!)
Was targeted by upperclassmen
Prowling for short-legged freshmen
Easily picked off in the generous
Hallways of the old stone architecture,
Which likewise included dank basement
Lairs like the one designated 'Senior
Lounge' where I was led by forceful
Palms clamped around my bony biceps.
Once the door shut, I was ringed by
Large boys aroused by their own cruelty.
Before they laid another hand on me,
My courage or fear plucked and I landed
A trifling blow on the chiseled shoulder
Of a future NFL superstar who grinned
Deviously as he self-selected to be my
Chief torturer and reached over my
Shoulder into my pants to grab a fistful
Of boxer short and pulled it viciously upward
With all his overdeveloped adolescent might

To the middle of my back, the ripping seams
Just the music he hoped for. He went on to
Lift me skyward like a tail-dangled puppy
And hooked the fabric onto an open locker
Door, so I hung humiliated and butt-bloodied
In a sad disfiguration of the hung man icon
(*In Cruce Glorior!*) I had been made to kneel
Before since toddler age. Over the next few
Eternal minutes, they spat, ogled, jeered,
Chuckled, probed, and otherwise brutalized
Me like the sacrificial lamb I had been taught
To venerate. The fabric finally gave and the
Gang released me into the upper realm
Of rigorous academics and befuddling
Theology where I tiptoed my way to
A stall and gingerly coaxed the cotton
Out of my numb and pounding asshole.
When the shaking lessened and I could
Halfway breathe again, I shuffled fifteen
Minutes late into religious studies class,
Sliding painfully into my seat red-faced
And ghost-eyed. I murmured an apology
And didn't mention my descent to the
Chamber of hell fire. The black-robed
Jesuits who ran and still run the school
Were sleepily aware of these and much
Worse goings on among the celebrated
Boys of Gonzaga High, especially after
Hours in the parks and streets of the city,
Brash destruction and violent abuse
Surreptitiously written into the strange
Social code of that male world. To this

Day, they persist in parading the motto
That once rose in the heated imagination
Of a well-meaning priest whose fantasy of
Maturing, selfless school lads is ironically
Emblazoned on their T-shirts and hats and
Distorted self-image: MEN FOR OTHERS.
Jesus, who would dare herald such a claim?

REMINDERS

It is our nature to lose sight of all that
Is brilliant. It is our charge to remind one
Another. That's one way of describing love.
To startle your lover into awakening.
Or to be started from a dream into the
Further dream of lovemaking in a dark
Open-windowed room. Or to find fresh flower
Petals scattered upon the breakfast table.
Or a hand gently slid into your own,
Making the moment when you thought
You were waiting for its arrival.

CAESURA

In the still of the half-empty cathedral,
There is only the light rise and fall
Of your torso pressed beside me.
In tandem with the singers, we
Take in a breath, and they begin,
A Hildegardian chant pooling
Generously around our bodies.

A decade before, we sat side by side
On that marbled sanctuary and made
Our bright-cheeked promise to
Whatever gods grace the union of
One to another. Perhaps our children
Stood dimly lit in the ranks, imagining
Their future lives.

Somewhere a primal star turns over
And burns out, finally given to the
Great blackness. Here it is our turn
To burn briefly with life, to let the music
Lap over us, to feel the approaching
Thunder outside rumble our chests,

To be drawn in and out of awarenesses,
The vision of who we are clouded
And cleared; and to breathe, delicately,
Together as our hair slowly silvers
And our juices leisurely ripen to a
Sweetness fit to one day be released
Into the dark earth.

POP
upon the death of my father

Men like you are hard to come by.
The world guts us of the qualities
You upheld to the end:
To keep your word, to honor your kin,
To give away your extra, then give again,
To endure trials, to track the necessary miles,
To be present to whatever life presented.
This was you; this was your way.
Old-fashioned is often well fashioned.
Modest and unflashy, heroes are thusly made.

Loss and grief nipped at your heels,
Fear and anger entangled your heart,
Yet you kept on, faithful to the song
Of your life that sounded through the years
And defied your secret fear that you would,
Like your father, leave too early,
Miss your children clutching diplomas and
Bearing wedding bands. Rather, as father,
You stood witness to it all, death did not call
Its claim for you. You lived and lived well
And I recall the facets of your genius.

A baseball pitcher, a master of trajectory,
In older times a legendary hunter you
Might have been. So each son and daughter
Was carefully taught the art of throwing
A ball, to hit the mark was cooked into
Our blood as native instinct. As was
Command of language, to stand before
The court or congregation, to move the
Hearts and spark the minds of a council
Or a lover, this too we learned from you.

Time flashed in untraceable shudders and
One by one five children set out your door
And one by one they brought ten grandchildren
To grace the threshold of your country home;
You wondered how long your luck could last
Until at last the body began to fail, to silently
Unravel and begin its solemn descent.
The will continued, unrelenting, your smile
Flashed and eye twinkled in cover of the mounting
Pain and the unshakeable summons from the
Gods of underworlds. When the ancestors
Came to ask for your death song, the tune
Rose sweetly and freely to your lips—
Oh Danny Boy, the pipes, the pipes are calling
From glen to glen and down the mountainside—
The verses were heard by unknown nurses
Who held your arm to guide you rightly home.

All your people gather around you now,
Bound by blood or heart, by labor or pleasure,
By religion or leisure, we are your sons and daughters,
Your soul's darling partner, your brothers, your
Colleagues, your clients, your athletes, your admirers
And contestants. All these have come.

To feel the air ringing with your dignity,
To see you off like an Irish king, to behold
You wink one last time and stride elegantly
Through the western sunset out into the
Blinking stars where you now belong and
Hold a place equal to your noble stature.

HAND TO HAND

I reach out and it's your hand stretched before me,
Dad, the grain and hair and warmth of skin so deeply
Known. Now I stand as father, my son before me, needing
Anything I can spare after proffering what the world requires.

I've learned to reserve the best for him, my boy, and his
Sisters, for his mother, and for my mother now widowed
And unsteadied. How is it, having died, you live newly in me?
I am pregnant with an agency—foreign yet familiar—
Something of your essence resurrected in me.

I never knew how to find someone past the grave, even
The seeking always felt empty. But, in graced moments,
You are undeniably finding me; I feel you speak with my
Tongue, love through my eyes, reach with my hand.

Last week, I was drawn to the filing drawers and pulled
A letter you wrote twenty-seven years ago, untouched since
Its first reading. I was then beginning my adult life, tasked
As a teacher and basketball coach at a faraway tribal school.

The letter was a bequest, your wisdom from coaching me
And my siblings and many others. Page after page, sketches
And figures and side annotations, guiding me, advising me,
Showing me, I too could lead a group, could inspire and tend
A pack of boys hungry to enter the arena.

Now each day I look for you, eager to feel you there, not in
Memory but in the living moment. In the wilderness of
Dreamtime. In the undocumented wonder of one bodiless
Soul loving its kin from within their grieving hearts.

There is a comfort there. Knowing, bodily now, the line of Ancestry is illuminated and empowered with each death. Somehow, and increasingly, I am you, Dad, and you are me.

FALLING
for my mother

In the last year of his life,
Dad fell in love with you all
Over again. So smitten did
He seem you were nearly
Overwhelmed with the
Daily declarations and hand-
Holding and sweet smiles.
Yet, it was exactly what your
Woman's heart needed and
Wanted after the speedy
Decades of not being seen or
Felt quite enough. And he fell
Toward you one final time,
Leaning down the basement
Stairs, calling for you and,
Not hearing a response, unable
To resist the instinct to guard
You from any harm. The framed
Images of the Beloved Mother
On the wall gazed kindly upon
Him as he tumbled into the dark
Stairwell, which began his descent
Into the next world. Perhaps the
Body collapses to humus and the
Soul rises. Or perhaps down and
Up aren't germane at all. Death
Must rather be a breaking open,
A release, an issuing out. Like
Water, like air. Which is where
You find him now: in your breath,
Easefully moving in and out of
Your aching lungs, kneading you

From the inside, loving you still.
For now it's you that's falling.
Fifty-four years of marriage
Abruptly and unalterably
Terminated has you often
Hurtling through cold space
With no ground to hold you in
Place. The earth will always pull
You back toward the comfort of
Its soft soil. Each dawn, awaking,
You find your breath yet in motion,
Quietly surrounding your heart,
Assuring you that somehow
All is okay. Whether you rise from
The bed or remain supine for hours,
Whether you feel devastated or
Numb or nothing at all, you are
Simply with it. As he is with you.
But newly. With no body or words,
He nudges you forward. To live
Again. In your time. In your way.
He needs nothing from you.
Only to see you smile once in
A while and to stay near when
You must weep. There is nothing
To accomplish. You have already
Done more than most. Just be.
Who you are blesses what
We who love you are becoming.

PULSE

GREEN MAN

I keep seeing him, some green man, some guide
Ahead who knows this wild earth far better

Than me. He glides light-footed along the steep
Slopes where I blunder through. The animals

Eye me puzzlingly where they nuzzle to him
And point their snouts toward nearby water

And warm bedding. The me of men and urbanity
Is a fool following this master of the wilds. His

Lips are often curled in a sly smile and his eyes
Carry the beam of moonset magic. I'd go with him

Anywhere, just to hear how he speaks to trees
And behold him fall to his knees at every fresh

Flowing fountain. He says the mountain birthed
Him and will claim him again one day, all things

Go home at last. He seems sturdy as an old boulder,
And the way he tells it, his body has been broken

And pieced together many times. He is the one
I go to sit with by firelight to hear his strange

Myths and riddling verses that spin me every
Which way. His recounts are unblemished by the

City mind and often reduce to just growls and
Snarls that lull me to the deeps. He himself sat

Years with an old woman who made medicines
From plants and read the dreamings of the stars.

She foretold it would become like this one day,
Brutal storms and ferocious wildfires and a sense

We'd lost our way. But the tellers of her girlhood
Spoke of humanity's underground past, and of

Seabound ages, insisting we have plenty of animal
Still in us. I know where I'll go when the walls

Begin to crumble. To the mountain, to clasp
Hands with my green man who knows the shape

Of nothingness and will without delay kneel down
And scratch the marks of a new plan into the dirt.

FOREST FOR US

I'm sat in the sticks, in the
Justness of all that's before me:
Gold eyelashed grasses, the
Jagged peak above, conifer
Roots below, love-entangled,
Holding the soil that holds me
In the freedom of the forest
Freely given for us to appreciate
And reciprocate with whatever
We can manage, our breath and
Our sweat at least, then a long
Glance to assess the damage.
Decades of pillage, decades of
Neglect, we'd do best to enter
On our bellies, heads down,
Hands out to the trees who are
Deep bereaved, parched or
Diseased, stumped or choked
By us, the chump who broke the
Natural laws one by one, we shot
Down the hoofed and the pawed
Without pause to gain permission
Or give thanks, so thanks to us
This forest is dwindling, elder-less
And swimming in our fumes
And our sprays, trees stuck
Fighting the men who breathe
From them, for once again our
Madness precedes us, the myopic
Species who poisons what feeds
Us. Are we hopeless, merely a

Future layer in the crust, famous
Just because we executed our own
Extinction, indulged ourselves to
Death? Or is something else afoot,
Some turnaround for good, some
Twist waiting in the bush, poised
To pounce and shake us around,
Pop us in the jaw, kick us in the
Rib, then kiss us up and down, lay
Us belly up to the clouds so we
Won't miss the new story drifting
In, dribbling down, kicking up
A beauty breeze through trees'
Limbs and over rocks' rims, a
Mighty keen retelling of the scene,
A pageless book being cooked
In us now to be served out our
Mouths as a wee medicine for the
Weakened heart of earth whose
Pulse is the thump beneath all,
The primeval lift and fall, the boom-
Boom of this signature place, this
Tiny blue grace laced together
Implausibly, each of us cells in a
Soil body whose glory nobody
Can contain or calculate and
Whose purpose is held before us,
To include us or consume us.
Both are possible see but there's
No telling which is what or who
Is we, but as for me I'm going
To take my chances in the trees,

For the forest is the furthest I
Can sink into the primary truth
Of my foot in the soil, of my feet
Become soil, fossilizing down as
A fuel or a bedrock for the fools
Or the wizards whose world will
Proceed ours, maybe redeem ours,
Smooth the gnarled scars and begin
Again, however it can: with a bang
Or a whimper and the glimmer of
A thing that's never been *(boom-*
boom) but has to be on behalf of the
Greater we, the all of it, so may we
Never quit working at it, feeling for
Our place and refining the face of
Humanity *(boom-boom)*, the people,
We are a strand in the web of life
That yet holds as a whole yet whose
Fate is unknown so let's hope to
Be shown how to go *(boom-boom)*
Or to stay *(boom-boom)* by a tree
(boom-boom) and just breathe…
(boom-boom, boom-boom, boom-boom)

DIRT ON OUR HANDS

Turn the dial back and back to
Before we were farmers, when
The soil was just forming from
The rock and the bone, a dark
Loam collected and connected
Root to root, worm to worm,
Piled up and plumped out into
The soft foundation of every
Civilization that's since risen
And fallen; it's all in the dirt, the
Record of earth now sounding
An alert 'cause we've run the same
Agrarian script too many times,
Aggrandized its scope to grotesque
Size and we're still at it, blasting
The ground, demanding more
Yield, blazing fields on bare stone,
Strong arming microbial drones
To produce rich topsoil and new
Oil from nothing but gumption
And the will of our self-centric
Dysfunction. But the figures are in,
The data are clear, we're tipping
Damn near to a fearsome topple
Down of an empire, fiercer than
Ever, with no space for refuge and
Recover; every river valley is spent,
Every mountain exhausted, the
Seas all diseased, the trees de-
Networked, the bottom line is zero:
Nothing and nowhere are the paired
Remnants of our legacy that we

Refuse to see though it's plain in
The clay beneath, bequeathed to
Us but squandered to dust and just
About gone, blown out beyond
Our reach, our perverse touch
Being leached from the fibers as
They sail out into the care of
Wherever they can settle and stay
And even lay the grounding for
The browning and greening of some
Good star perhaps luckier or abler
Than ours. Or at least free of
Concrete and cars, innocent to
Conquest and guards guarding
Counterfeit lines in the sand
When it was the land who needed
Protecting, but we left her uncovered,
Denuded then smothered with
Synthetics till her skin cracked
And crumbled into clumps all
Pithless and pathetic, desiccated to
Mostly dead. So if we're here with
The last of this inimitable base, may
We have the grace or the pluck to
Plant ourselves in the soil and find
Out what we're really made of. At the
Very least our last act would be love.

ELEPHANTS

This is our grace: to be a note in the exact chord that animates creation.
—The Elephants (as heard by Deena Metzger)

The elephants spoke truly so duly may
We each play our note and become our
Grace, our feet laced by the sand of
Wherever we stand in that just-right
Chord which accords to the key of wind
Whipping flame through the understory
Of all we've left untended in this demented
Era where we dismissed elephants and so
Many others then smothered the earth mother
With our countless demands until one has
To wonder how the ancestors must weep
As our blunders increase and the inheritance
They prepared for us and kept safe is pared
Down and erased. But life has reduced to
Nothing before, so the old ones sagely stored
The finest seed pebbles they had in the
Breastpocket of a thundergod whose given
Nod will broadcast that bounty about, but
Without a soft moist base to shore those
Pebbles here, it would all be for naught.
So we're caught in the spotlit heat, lockset
In the hinge of a great turning for which
The warnings have been plainly delivered:
In the shiver-shakes of core plates, in the
Lifting of seas and the falling of forests,
In the hardening of soils and the exodus
Of insects; it's all kept asking us to rejoin
The song that's sung earth along since before
Lungs and a tongue were shaped in the first
Human who found when they uttered the
AH and the OHM and the HU that magic

Crackled the air, but that same magic worked
Backward looses demons asprawl who yowl
In delight when we transpose the natural
Music of praise to a degraded refrain of
Transactional speech that fears anything
Wild unless it's drowsed and corralled.
Now either the cages are sprung or we are
To be hung from the science trees we grafted
And grew to shade us from the hot truth
Of a world made by us for us that sucks
At the sources of life till it will swallow itself
Whole and leave only ghosted wisps of what
Was when we were notes in the chord that
Called forth the rain, colored the sky,
Fruited the vines, hatched the eggs, greened
The hills, foamed the seas, and made the
Elephants trumpet because it all fit together
In a beauty so astounding that every being
Couldn't help but sing; so sing out fellow
Humanoids, for the droids are watching and
Waiting to see if we'll manage to keep a seat
On this blue sphere. Let's pause at the
Crossroads and let the elephants pass through
Into the newness of what might be before us
When it's no longer all for us but assured by
Us, if we give our keen minds wholly over to
The holy spark holding steady in the heart
Of the dark earth core that sustains all this
Clay-water-air preciousness, pressing us on
To the clarity now dawning in so many and
Soon occurring to so many more who must

Wake for this fever to break, for earth to shake
Off the skin that died and expose a bright
Pulp one layer farther into the unplumbable
Profundity that curiously keeps keeping us
Around, gravity-bound, love-drowned,
Heads in the stars and toes on the ground.

CULTURE

All cultures of earth found their birth
In nature, humans attuning to the genius
Of place, case by case, we shaped our
Homes to fit the land, filled our bellies
With the plants at hand, found our stories
And songs in the long trails between
Watersheds, bedding down in starlight
Or rainfall, awake to it all. A culture
Thusly made is real, honest and robust,
Ever replenished by the new season,
The new moon, the tune and timbre of
The forest pouring through us, as sure as
Our breath, fluid until death; yet the death
Of these same cultures came not from
The wilds but the guile of unsure humans
Coercing other humans to foster a sinister
Second nature that kills what it fears, that
Tears apart anything deemed other, as if
The earth mother weren't one complete
Being, as if injury to her torso doesn't
Weaken her dorsal. People upon people
Stamped out other different people and
Languages, as if this elevated the stampers'
Tongue rather than dampening the total
Sound. The same mindset was aimed at
Nonhuman species. We cheaply bartered
Natural biodiversity for an engineered
Uniformity so unsteady it's been forcibly
Upheld by warfare—physical-economic-
Ecologic warfare—wherefore the losses are
Immeasurable and escalate exponentially
Over time. So how can we unwind all we've

Tangled, collect the dangled remnants of
Lost cultures, or live without culture, or
Build culture back from scratch? We must
Return to wild nature. Sit by the stream
Till our blood runs clean, till our trained
Minds retreat and our squeezed hearts ease
And we again hear the trees speak, touch
Moss to our cheek, sense deer sensing us,
Feel storms as they form, wake to the
Unmistakable enchantment all around,
Calling us to fall back into our place, as
Tenders of fire, keepers of water, dignified
Peoples whose manner of hunting and
Planting, of feasting and dancing delights
The gods, regards the animals, follows the
Stars, and feeds the thunders, the rainmakers
And snowbringers who are the true
Orchestrators of earthly life. Might we speak
The language of lore rather than lists;
Might we thread our way creek to creek
More than street to street; might our
Lovemaking overtake our career-making;
Might our lives be guided by the rule of
Paradox above absolutes; and might death
Be known as so alluring we hunger for
Our turn to drop into otherworlds, disappear
Into the curl of a stream, into the shade of
A dream we left waiting…in such
Reimagined environs, culture will gently
Rise, surmise, invigorate, and propagate for
A long, long while. Until we kill it again.
As has always been the way from before

Humans appeared and will be after humans
Are cleared and composted and all falls
Back to nothingness. Which is simply
Everything burned down, collected as ash,
Held holy for a broad pause, then reconstituted
By a raindrop, a sunbeam, and a thin breeze.

HER WE SERVE

What can even be said in this weak bread of English
That's just a mishmash of post-colonial backlash and
Bears only a quarter of the sounds of any live indigenous
Tongue that might've once run in every human mouth,
But now we've cut our speech down to a monocrop of
Ameri-corporate sound that's barked outta the dark
Jaws of the tech hounds who got infected then let the
Spoiled genome roam so we all bit the bait and ate the
Potion of a pseudo-intelligence that now runs all the
Souped-up virtual engines that keep us sunken down,
Drunken clowns who keep falling further down rabbit
Holes yet don't even feel the soil in this communal
Mind swirl; our senses blasted, we're cast in concrete
Then stacked like blocks and stuck in boxes so we can't
Quite get our heads straight and start to violate the real
Mandates. Who is this monster terrorizing the water,
Terrified of fire, spitting poison all over the sky, taking
And taking and taking and never waking to a give-back,
A script flip, a gift that goes for once from us to earth?
She hurts so much with love for us but never once did
I see a priest sign his hand over the land, a president
Tip his hat to the sun, a general wave the flag of plant
Nation, a white-coat doctor shrug and ask Great Mystery
What's wrong, a Wall Street suit follow the pulsing ticker
Tape of northern flicker song. Maybe it's this English
That's smellin' foul, just look at how it spread continent
To continent in a nonorganic oral implantment, mouth
To mouth forced upon peoples who were breathing fine,
Now made to shape their breath out of nature's time and
Give their lips to an awkward rhyme, then innocently pass
It on to their kids and hide the old sounds and songs and
Conversation with beasts and thunders and woodland

Wonders, silencing the wild and denying every child what
Was once and might've been if we'd remembered then the
Only intellect that knows is the one who goes to the cave
To hear secrets told, seeks their knowing from the stars'
Glowings, takes their verbals after the sea burbles, and never
Forgets to sprinkle corn or herb in exchange for whatever's
Heard or shown or given; for what isn't gift after all, and it's
Tragical how we trash it all, bury our plastic and pipe our
Poop when we could bury a seed and feed it with leavings
From us and all the rest—can we ever clean this mess?
Maybe the English can be cleaned too, brought through
To a new standing. I dunno, let's lie flat and ask the fungi
How to speak, ask the roots to teach, ask the clay for a
Way out or ahead or somekinda'where where we bear our
Words with a beauty that becomes the magic of a tongue
That flicks out the spells of a world gone well, an earth not
For sale that sails in the stars and is ours as we're hers
For it's her that we serve.

WHAT IT IS

Residual traumas
Are rising on t-shirts
And spilling on sneakers
And filling the streets up
The kids they are yearning
And what they are learning
Is everything 'round them
Is gonna be burning
The CEOs lying
So people keep buying
The new stuff and new stuff
It keeps multiplying
We're locked in our houses
Like skittish brown mouses
We eat and we eat more
For nothing will rouse us
Our bodies are tired
Our minds are cross-wired
The media blitzkrieg
It got us blindsided
We don't feel the sunlight
We prefer our screens bright
We won't drink the water
Not treated and sealed tight
Our cultures have vanished
Our traditions banished
We're hunting for food for
Our souls that are famished
We can't speak the old tongues
We're coded by strange ones
Invisibly morphing
Every millisecond

All managed by robots
Who spin us into knots
Until we've all forgot
What life is and is not
Splash water on our faces
To wake us and make us
Follow the traces
Of ancestors' ways, it's
The least we can do
To replant what they grew
To fix what we broke
Clear the sludge and the smoke
Of our unholy fires
That never expire
Keep consuming and ruining
The garden once blooming
Now waiting in silence
For the violence to die out,
The madmen to lie down,
The engines to quiet,
The dollars to sour,
The trees to reflower
The land with a fragrance
That heals all our flagrant
Foils and despoils,
All our doom and our gloom,
All the stress and the mess,
Let earth rest and reset
Then she'll cast out her net
To the stars to bring in
What we need to begin
The healing the repair

The youth are aware
Of where this might go
So they stand to declare:
Some good could be next
Let's expect what is best
Let's respect and connect
With the deep intellect
That thrums in our blood
That drums in our hearts
That hums in our minds
Reminds us to serve
All life for all time
Reminds us to serve
All life for all time
Reminds us to serve
All life for all time

MA SAYS

Ma says, Be happy
Ma says, Be still
Ma says, Now come close
Ma says, I'm ill

Ma says, Take comfort
Ma says, Have trust
Ma says, But hear me
Ma says, You must

Act on my behalf
Speak for me now
Little time remains
So I'll tell you how

I'll show the way
I'll provide the means
Just tell me you're willing
Come toward me please

Step onto my breath
Enter my body
In the dark of my belly
I'll remake you fully

I'll hold you inside
The secret of secrets
Repair your mind
Reclaim you as my child

I chose you long ago
Plucked you from the stars

Dropped you in the dirt
Mixed you with my spit

Patted you together
Breathed you into being
This is your story
Lean into its meaning

In your eyes I scripted
The star charts you need
These are the instructions
All can be redeemed

The quickening within you
The urgency you feel
Must be attended
The climacteric is real

Yet a magnificence exists
At the center of the storm
Stand firm and soon
You will glimpse its form

You will feel its beat
Awaken in the soil
Pound like thunder
Shake loose your soul

Ma says, We cannot wait
Ma says, The time is now
Ma says, Take courage
Ma says, Make the vow

To give yourself over
To leave your old house
To walk out with nothing
To make Ma your spouse

Come to the mountains
Sit by the creek
In the center of the forest
You will hear me speak

I am right beside you
Ever am I yours
The earth is my temple
Without ceiling or doors

When you sing my name
I'm with you
When you dance
I'm whirling too

Ma says, I need you
More than ever, says Ma
I go before you
Come and follow Ma

BEING HELD

I have seen a large stone lodged within a tree,
though really the tree grew around the stone,
stone and tree each being what they are:
unrelenting and, by degrees, softening.

Likewise, my heart may have leaned into
the flying arrow that now sits in soft tissue,
incriminated and then embraced.

So all things hold their place yet yield
to the great wholeness.
All postures of reverence fall away.
One seed is planted, another eaten.

To be held, as the earth finally holds us,
both earth and us thereby enlarged,
is everything.

MYTH

NEW QUEEN, NEW CHILDREN

I'm told there's a new queen under the hill.

It's said her face blurs before the beholder
like a dream image, and that none can quite
catch her eye. I hear she seems ever on the go,
a long shock of hair trailing down her back.

By all reports, she's been here all along but
walked unseen among us, waiting for the time
to step forward, to seize the scepter, to rise.
Nobody recalls just how she took hold of the

palace or where she assembled the scores of
many-shaped, every-colored women who now
scurry about its grounds with firm intent and
no time for the usual flirtations. They and their

queen carry the polish of elevated status but
with no apparent wealth. There hasn't been war
there in years, but it's sworn the clang of swords
rings out in the deep of night from the upper

floors. And, at dawn, women on horseback are
seen trotting in from the forest, often with meat
draped over the saddles, and always with a keen
knowing about them. It's not certain if they are

the ones foretold in the old tales, but I am
prepared to find out. I've packed my satchel and
donned my cloak and will voyage many days to
that subterranean fortress. Whatever is happening,

it's going to change everything, and I cannot stay
away. I've seen it all in my dreams: the collapse
and the revival, a melee of tempestuous flames
and broken bloodlines. Followed by the green

shoots of a master food grown from seeds long
held underground. And, whether I live to glimpse
them, the hauntingly prismatic eyes of the next
children, wise beyond telling, fierce beyond measure,

risen from soil to bravely steer the way forward.

THE YOUNG MAN AND THE CRONE

Once there was and once there was not a mountainside village of tents and small huts where a marvelous band of people made their home over the generations. Being mountain people, they were attuned to the seasons and weather of their place, intimately familiar with the land's contours and features, dependent upon its edible gifts, its rich soil, its clear water. And in happy alliance with the animals of the locale, often crafting gifts to take on their hunts.

For they were also a hunting people. And on most full moon evenings, especially when the hunters were home, sometimes with fresh meat, the villagers gathered around the open fire and shared food and story and song. And danced together, giving thanks for their communal life and praying for its continuation.

In the village, there was once a young man like and unlike the others. He was a good hunter. He was partnered with a beautiful and dignified woman who bore the couple several delightful, if rambunctious, children. He was respected among the people and had everything he needed. Yet he longed for something he lacked. For on those full moon gatherings, he always stood back in silence. When others stood as tellers or singers, his insides ached. He yearned to know the feeling of a song in his throat or a story ablaze in his imagination. And when the drumming began, he felt stiff and awkward, so different from the graceful way he moved on the hunt. No one, not even his woman, knew quite how much his constriction of voice and body tormented him.

One winter evening, the day before a hunt was arranged, a massive snowstorm drifted in and loomed behind the peaks. The hunt was canceled. The next morning, snow fell steadily, yet the day was bright and inviting, so the man felt the urge to take a wander in the nearby hills he knew so well. He gathered a small bundle of essentials and made his way up toward his favorite canyon. As he climbed, he fell deeply into his thoughts and did not sense the weather turning.

Suddenly, a great mist swept in and was fully upon him. In moments, everything was obscured in thick wet whiteness. He scrambled up, seeking a point of visibility, yet the cover was impenetrable. Quickening his step, he stumbled on a snow-covered stone and fell headlong. When he rose, the landscape had mysteriously shifted and felt foreign and unrecognizable. Somehow, he had been pulled into an otherworld, one not obliged to the usual laws of nature.

Again and again, he tried to climb out of the canyon but only succeeded in descending farther into its depths. He finally stopped moving and attempted to light a fire with his worn and trusted kit of sticks. But there was no ignition in it this night. And every stick around him was thickly frozen underneath what looked like months of ice. A wave of despair hit him squarely in the gut. For the first time in his life, he called out in desperation, hopelessly shouting into the freezing winds.

Only the echo of his own voice was heard in response. The man urgently considered the situation. Dusk had arrived and he could no longer see well enough to walk. His hands and feet were entirely numbed so building a snow shelter seemed impossible. The only choice was to simply keep his body in motion and hope it generated enough heat to survive the night. So, he began to step, lifting each foot in turn, over and over. A couple hours into it, his extremities began to warm slightly and he felt a tinge of promise. Again, he called out into the darkness to anything that might be near. This time, there was an uncanny sense that something heard him.

From nowhere, an old crone appeared between the trees and approached him. As she came near, he saw her fierce ice-blue eyes, her wild tangled hair, her torn garments. He knew this was no human woman. This was an enchanted being, a spirit of the forest, that must be given offerings. He lay down the remnants of his food and water upon the forest floor, then added a packet of medicinal herbs and a pebble bracelet from his wrist. It was all he had. And he knew the bargain was serious.

The crone came close enough to speak. *"Because you honored me with gifts, I will help you. I will give you a choice. Either I light a path all the way up the mountain for you to follow home and sleep this night with your woman and children. Or you stay here for three nights and three days, come what may. And, if you survive, I will give you a song."*

The man was terrified. And invigorated. He knew what he should do. His family awaited him, needed him. Yet his longing was so strong. To live and never know the feel of a song in the throat seemed unbearable. Oddly, he felt he had waited his entire life for this very opportunity. As he uttered his response, his whole body bristled with energy. "I will stay."

"Unfasten your foot coverings and give them to me," rasped the crone.

Without reason, he trusted her and unlaced his tall deer-hide foot wraps and laid them out on the snow. The crone slyly scooped them up, then turned and disappeared.

The storm raged, ten times harsher than before. Winds ripped through. Snow became sleet and the land froze over. The man was forced to begin stepping upon the icy ground. The cold increased and his steps became more vigorous. He was exhausted, yet if he wavered, his body began to shudder violently. In that desperately spent state, his stepping found a rhythm and it was clear, for the first time ever, he was *dancing*. For his life. And he continued all night, dancing and dancing just to keep his heart awake. Years and years of missed dances were accounted for through that long cold wet night.

When dawn finally came, the sun rose very rapidly and its welcome warmth quickly intensified to an unnatural heat. In minutes, all the ice was gone and the land and trees began to bake in the now blistering temperatures. All the man could do was lay on the earth in the narrow shade of a pine tree, floating in and out of consciousness, able only to feebly bring the scorched air in and out of his lungs. The day was eternal. The heat unrelenting. Until, finally, the sun dropped beneath the horizon and the second night engulfed the man.

Again, the storms, the mist and sleet and freezing winds. Again, his naked feet stepped upon the ice, burning with the cold, then reduced to numb cumbersome blocks. But he never stopped. He danced and danced until again dawn broke. The second day was as excruciating as the first. And the third night as brutal as the other two. Yet when dawn came for the third time, the crone faithfully appeared, backlit by a brilliant light that obscured her face.

She approached the man and came close, very close, then opened her wrinkled, whiskery, broken-toothed mouth and placed it roughly upon the man's cracked and ravaged lips and breathed into him a huge gust of spruce-scented air. *"Now you have a song,"* she squawked. Then turned and again disappeared into the trees. And a path all the way up the mountain came aglow. Beside it, the man's foot coverings sat freshly oiled and gleaming.

The man broke his spot of three nights and gingerly walked to the path, fastened his coverings to his thawing feet, and began to ascend. As he walked, a strange feeling quickened in his belly. The sensation spread throughout his body. It was utterly novel yet felt so right, so luscious and compelling. *Surely, this was the song.* Without forethought, he found his mouth opening and sounds emerging and forming a melody. He was indeed, singing! *Singing!* He sang the song to its end. Then sang it again. And again. Over and over, all the way up the mountain and to the village. He dared not stop for fear of forgetting it.

As he neared the village, a young boy saw him coming. He ran to tell the people. All were astonished. In the village, the storm had been vicious and unceasing. There had been no heat or melting in the daytime for them, just perpetual snow and sleet. So the man's funeral had been prepared. The elders were presently gathered in a ceremonial lodge making the prayers to send his soul home. Instead, the frail, yet living, man was brought into the lodge and doctored by the village healer. He was then brought to the healer's hut and laid before the fireplace where he slept like the dead for three days.

When he emerged, a fire was ablaze in the village center. A huge celebration had been arranged. And when it came time for the merriment to turn toward music and sharing, the young man stepped forward. And sang the song. The tones of his voice were hauntingly beautiful. The villagers were rightly spellbound. When the last note rang out, all who listened were deeply satisfied. And the man finally knew what it was to give a song to his people.

And then the drumbeats began to roll over the assembly. The man walked to his woman and extended his hand. She was in disbelief. Was he asking her to dance? They walked hand in hand to the circle and the man began to step with grace and ease. The woman smiled widely and fell into his lead, the two spinning and curving as one for hours together.

For the next several turns of the moon, the man was asked to sing the song again. Each time, it was better. Richer, more satisfying. His voice became liquid and increasingly nimble. And each full moon, he danced. With his woman as well as in the men's formations. He belonged to his people in a way that had previously seemed impossible.

On the thirteenth full moon after his return, rather than sing, the man told the story of his ordeal in the canyon in full detail. This caused the council of elders to confer long into the night. Some of them had heard their great grandparents speak of the old crone. She was a formidable presence.

The next day, the man was brought to the village center where the healer stood holding a small wrapped bundle. He unfolded it to reveal a string of wolf's teeth. This necklace was placed over the man's head. And the healer spoke, "She will come to you again in the forest. Wear this always for protection. She will sense it, even beneath your garments, and do no harm to you. Gift her. And feed her well."

As far as is known, the man ventured deep into the mountains each winter to meet the crone and receive another song. All year, he prepared his gift for her, usually carving designs into a chosen tree limb for he learned of the crone's fondness for carved wands. Their arrangement was mutual and fair, if dangerous and abnormal. Yet always the man felt indebted to her.

So, one winter, now well into his old age, the man walked up into the hills with no food and no gifts and without the wolf's teeth necklace and laid himself down as the gift. And the crone was instantly upon him and hungrily ate him to the last bone.

THE WELL OF ELOQUENCE

In an older time, on an island thickly forested with oak and pine, an intricate oral culture developed among the islanders who spoke an ancient tongue little remembered in this day and age. There was a young gentleman who carried the name Tadhg, meaning storyteller or poet, and his heart was true to the moniker. For he dearly loved all the tales of his people's lore, all their rhyming verses and long poems, and their many songs and tunes. He had a perfect memory and held all this material firm in his heart.

But Tadhg had an ill-starred affliction. There was a twist in his tongue that prevented him from speaking fluently. He would instead stammer and stutter and muffle his words in his mouth. Inside, though none knew it, he held a vast treasure of poetry and myth and history.

One fine spring evening, at the very end of storytelling season, the teller of his town recounted a well-loved tale about the legendary Well of Eloquence, the spring which was the headwaters of the largest river on the eastern coast of the island. As the teller came to the story's end which declared that anyone who drank of this special well in the month of June would live the poet's life, Tadhg's entire body shivered with excitement. For he knew he must go to the Well of Eloquence and drink of its pure water.

That very evening, he began to plot out his journey, which would involve a high mountain crossing and long days in deep forests. He surmised the pilgrimage would take several weeks to complete. He departed the following week, on the first day of June, at dawn, carrying what he could manage as far as provisions and hunting tools.

He traveled nearly a week through networks of forests until he came to the big mountain range in the center of the island. Each night, he lit a fire and would silently pore through the oral lore that lived in him, inwardly enjoying all that verbal richness. After another week, he made it over and down the mountains into the final stretch of the voyage. After twenty-seven days walking, Tadhg finally made it to the village where the river originated and rose aboveground. He began to ask, as best he could in his brief stammers, about the well's precise location. Everyone to a person would not respond but merely glanced down at their feet as if they hadn't heard Tadhg's question.

Only one, known only as the Laughing Man by the locals of that region, had anything at all to say to Tadhg about the well. The Laughing Man chortled out, "It's the Well of Eloquence, you're after, is it? If you want to go there, you'll have to ask the king himself. And it's nigh impossible to be granted an audience with him!" And then he exploded into fits of laughter.

Distraught and befuddled, Tadhg wandered that evening in the woods that surrounded the central castle of the village. Only one day remained in the month of June. Despite all his efforts and genuine desire, he had failed to find the well. He found himself on a small hunting trail in the pines and thought at least he might catch a hare or other fine dinner before he turned back toward home. As he began to track the area, he heard a nearby disturbance and three dogs popped out of the bramble, followed by a well-dressed man. The man seemed surprised to find another person in this hunting area.

"What's your errand, boy?" he inquired of Tadhg.

Tadhg shook his head, afraid to speak to someone of the man's stature.

"Surely you're here with a purpose. Go on, say what it is you seek."

Tadhg again shook his head, bowed in apology, and turned to walk away.

The man softened his tone, "Come now, do not fear. Tell me what's on your heart."

Tadhg mustered his courage and the words came in short bursts, "I've come—to visit—the holy well—I wish—I wish—to—to be a bard."

"A bard now? Well, that's a noble pursuit. Is it just you, no one else?"

"Only me," Tadhg managed.

"Well, then. Do not go by the front gate. You'll arouse suspicion. There is a small gate on the north side of the castle built between two oak trees and concealed by ivy. Enter there. Follow the slope down to the river and upstream to its beginning. Go to the well and not beyond."

The man strode off, his dogs trotting alongside. Tadhg was stupefied. Surely this was both permission and instruction to enter the castle grounds. And just in time. As the light waned, Tadhg cut a feathery branch from an old yew tree to add to his bundle of offerings. For the story told of a goddess who lived at the well. A feminine being whose body was the river, whose hair was the flowing current, whose mouth was the well itself. And who would as soon swallow a man as bathe him in her waters.

That night, Tadhg slept little but dreamed much and rose well before dawn. By the time the sky began to fill with light, he was standing at the northern ivy-covered gate. He entered the grounds and made his way to the water whose rushing sound sent his heart aflutter. As Tadhg neared the well, which was protected by a small earthen enclosure, he stopped to prepare himself. He removed his hat and boots, set down his shoulder bag and removed his small pouch of offerings. He approached the well barefooted and circumambulated the earthen mound no less than nine times before he stooped down and knelt before the shadowed waters.

He laid his gifts at the lip of the well. He knew from the lore what most pleased a goddess. The yew branch he placed down first. Upon it, three small stones: one ruby-colored, one sapphire-hued, and one made of white quartz. Between these three, he set two deer toes. And sprinkled flower petals on top.

When all was set, he gazed a long while at the clear water until it sparkled in a way that felt like a welcome. Then Tadhg knelt forward, dipped his hands into that wet coolness, and brought it to his lips. He drank very deeply.

As the liquid ran down his gullet, he felt his tongue untwist and his throat open. He called out, at first with a hunter's whoop when the shot was true. His voice rang clear and full like never before. And then he began to speak. An old prayer. A poem. Another. A song. A story. It all poured forth. He spoke and spoke for hours at the well's edge, letting everything held so long inside emerge and vibrate in the clear air. Then Tadhg stood and began his new life.

He traveled the island from village to village as an itinerant teller, becoming more and more masterful with his verses and stories. He became known for his tendency not to take the roads but to move through the untracked woods and fields and to appear to people and at places suddenly, much like a wild animal. He was unmistakable with his thick red beard, his green felted hat, and his signature walking and speaking stick ever in his hand.

For nine years, he lived as a wanderer and teller. His travels eventually brought him back to the same eastern village where he had first set out from the holy well. To his surprise, on that day, the front castle gates were open. For the wedding feast of the king's daughter was being celebrated and all were welcome.

Tadhg entered and made his way to the main courtyard where the festivities were in full procession. In the very center of the action, the bride and groom stood with hands fasted together, and the king stood beaming behind them. Tadhg immediately recognized the king as the very man he had met in the woods nine years before. And the king too noticed a bard had arrived, attired in much the usual fashion but with a distinct gleam to him. So he bellowed, "Bard, give us a verse!"

The musicians played upon their stringed instruments and Tadhg began to sing with tremendous skill the long poem of his own journey. His pilgrimage to the well and his travels throughout the land. The king remembered him and was astonished at his well-honed skills of oratory. He gave Tadhg a permanent seat in the court as the royal bard.

Through the years, Tadhg rose to the highest rank of poet and was widely regarded. His name became much grander than himself and people now began to arrive on pilgrimage to see him. So as not to disappoint these hopeful and often desperate souls, Tadhg said little to the pilgrims and rather pointed them to the well, suggesting the remedies and insights they sought might lie there in the goddess' care.

When his beard had turned full white and his hair silvered, Tadhg felt it was time to depart the castle and retreat from society once more.

He packed a small bundle and made his way back toward the center of the island to a certain forest, which held a special ancient oak grove that was known to provide good entry to the underworld.

At the edge of the twisting, towering oaks, Tadhg put down his stick and hat, knelt to sniff the black humus, and then entered the grove with a light heart. If any beings of leg or wing were there, they beheld the marvel of a man walking into the dappled shadows and simply slipping between narrow folds of light.

THE BOY, THE BEAR, AND THE GOLD RING

Long ago, on a remote sea-wracked island, there lived a boy and his family. Their hut, like all the others in their village, was built of stone and mud. The surrounding conifer forests provided firewood to warm the homes and the people scratched a living from the stony soil as well as by wild harvesting roots and plants and by bow-hunting animals, small and large.

The boy, the eldest of four brothers, was named Thordis. He had just received his seven-year ceremony to mark completion of his early childhood. Everything felt right in the universe. And then one day, he awoke to hear his father coughing violently beside the fireplace. As he blinked his eyes awake, four men burst into the hut, bundled his father in blankets, lifted him and whisked him away into the cold morning.

The next time the boy and his brothers saw their father, he was lifeless, wrapped in a bear hide and placed onto a blazing pyre. He was magnificently adorned in the cloak of his clan, with his bow laid across his chest, his knife tied to his belt, and a metal neck ring perfectly shined for his meeting with the ancestors.

Thordis' younger brothers were in a state of innocence and graced numbness. Thordis, however, at seven years of age, realized the finality of his hero's departure. The pain of it landed in his heart like a nail driven deeply and ruthlessly. Each day seemed more unbearable than the next. He fell into a disillusioned state. He stopped playing with his brothers and the other boys. Then he stopped eating his meals. And finally, he even stopped speaking and walked the village like a ghost.

One moonless night, Thordis climbed a hillside above the village and sat alone in his desperation. He longed for the gods to bring his father back, for something to end the nightmare he was living. He rose from his spot and began to wander down into the hills. He dropped into a twisting gulley with a thin trickle of water and followed it down until it opened into a pond he had never come upon before.

The stars were brightly reflected upon the water's surface and Thordis crouched at the pond's edge. On the opposite side, a large creature slid out of the water and perched upon a submerged boulder. As Thordis' eyes focused, he identified what was surely the form of a bear upon the stone. The creature slipped back into the water and swam toward Thordis who was frozen in fear and anticipation. The beast emerged just inches before Thordis. It was indeed a giant blonde bear who opened his mouth widely to reveal a gold ring looped on its curved tooth.

Instinctively, Thordis plucked the ring from the bear's tooth and clasped it in his sweaty palm. The bear instantly dropped back into the water and swam off. Thordis glanced down and marveled at the sheen of the ring in his hand. When he looked up again, the bear had vanished. In fact, the boulder had vanished too. And the pond. Yet, the ring remained, solid and real as ever.

Thordis stood from his spot and began to climb back up the gulley. As he did so, the terrain began to look familiar again. In minutes, he had located what his people called the big trail which led to and from his village. He followed the smooth wide path all the way home. It was late but he slipped silently into the furs on his bedmat and slept deeply.

The next day, his mother, who had become increasingly worried about him, brought Thordis with her to a ceremony led by the village sage. They crawled together into the low windowless stone hut where the door was shut to make for total darkness. In the middle of the ritual, without warning, the old sage interrupted his chanting and rattling and suddenly spoke out, "The ring you carry makes the unseen seen. Use it wisely," then continued the chants and prayers.

That evening, Thordis slipped the ring onto his finger, hoping to see his father, and was instead flooded with a barrage of confusing and disturbing images. He pulled the ring quickly from his finger and dropped it into a special white deerskin bag his father had given him. He tucked the bag behind a loose stone in the wall and left it there.

When Thordis reached nine years, he was welcomed on the fall hunt. He would travel without a weapon and observe, as was the custom for boys of that age. However, he secretly brought the ring with him, and, on the first morning of the hunt, slid it on. This time, the imagery was calm and clear. He saw an antlered buck standing alone in a pine glade. Without forethought, Thordis leaped into action. He snatched an older boy's bow and quiver and sprinted into the woods. His feet moved beyond his will and took him directly to the place he had seen in vision. Several older boys followed on Thordis' heels, astonished at the gall and vigor upsurging from the usually sullen boy.

Thordis saw the buck and stopped short. With untrained skill, he pulled an arrow, notched it, lifted the bow, drew and held it steady. He whispered the words his father had told him the master hunters used, "Journey well. Return to us once more," and let the arrow fly. The shot was spot-on and the animal quivered and fell into a heap. Thordis ran to the body while the assembled crowd stood slack-jawed and flabbergasted. He touched his gold ring to the heart of the deer and breathed, "Thank you," before pulling the arrow from its lungs and walked off, leaving the carcass to be cut and dressed by the other hunters.

For weeks, the other boys begged Thordis to hunt again, but he refused and returned to his silent, morose ways. In fact, he became even more aloof and hardly interacted with anyone. Every so often, he would try the ring on again, but still he could not see or sense his father.

At age fourteen, Thordis had reached another threshold, eligible to be initiated into the ranks of manhood. He felt unprepared and visited the village sage alone, unmuting his voice to ask for a packet of mugwort dreaming tea. The older man sat awhile smoking his clay pipe in silence, and then asked, "Have you the ring still?" Thordis nodded. "It will guide you," rumbled the sage as he handed over the herbal mixture. That night, Thordis drank it, put on the gold ring, and went to sleep.

A dream came. In it, his father at last appeared to Thordis. He was, however, frail and emaciated, his hair matted, his body bound in knotted cords and writhing in agony. After some time, an odd sapphire-hued moon rose and poured a cascade of light over his father, scattering the cords and leaving him free, his hair now smoothed and his body restored, again tall and fleshy. As he strode off in his signature elegance, he turned his head back toward Thordis and smiled at him before disappearing.

The dream sequence then flashed to Thordis' mother. She wore her hooded cloak and stood before a place high in the hills the villagers called Blue Falls. There, she dropped to her knees and wept. And wept. She ripped at her hair and wailed. She thrust her head in and out of the water numerous times and coughed up a large black mass, then collapsed into the pool beneath the rushing falls. A few moments later, she surfaced and floated up onto her back, arms outstretched, and drifted slowly to the shore. When she rose to her feet, a great peacefulness was upon her.

When Thordis awoke, he also felt a change, as if a huge sack of stones had been lifted from his back. The dream brought comfort he hadn't felt since the day his father departed. Thordis slowly began to engage with his people again. He even decided he would join the fall hunt that year. All the men were delighted for they knew he carried a mysterious gift.

As before, Thordis secretly slipped on the ring during the first morning of the hunt. And, as before, he was shown a prize, this time a group of female elk grazing in a rocky meadow. Thordis took off in a sprint and was followed by numerous men, including the sharpest shooter of the village. Thordis reached a raging river and waded in without hesitation, knowing the meadow lay just across the waters. As he stepped into the wild waters, the frothy waves rushed over his hands and the gold ring shot from his finger into the current. And was gone.

Thordis felt his heart drop and cried out in anguish. His legs folded beneath him and his body rolled into the current. As his head went in and out of the frigid waters, he wondered if he should just let himself go and be taken by the river. His body was tossed about another moment or two, before something in him rose up and compelled him to swim for shore. He made it to the river's edge, heaving violently and spitting out water.

Back home, Thordis was again dejected and withdrawn, not eating or speaking. After a week, his mother became worried and visited the sage on her own. The old man decided Thordis needed the old initation rite of sitting out on the mountain for three nights. When Thordis' mother told him of the sage's instructions, he agreed to the initiation rite, thinking if he was meant to die, he could do so on the mountain.

The sage walked Thordis to the forest edge and left him there. Thordis stood motionless that night, simply staring ahead in an unfeeling daze. The next day, he sat upon the ground and stayed that way all day and into the night, thinking only of his lost ring, his lost father, his unshakeable grief. On the third day, he lay upon the humus and dreamed with the earth. When he awoke, a refreshment was in his heart and a quickening was in the air.

He quickly stood and scanned. Seeing little, he listened intently and heard a nearby rustling. A bear emerged between the trees and approached his spot. Thordis stood steady. He knew it was the blonde bear who had given him the ring.

The bear raised onto his hind legs and touched his snout to Thordis' nose and breathed heavily upon him. Thordis felt his own body lengthen and sprout fur and claws. He stood snout to snout with the bear for a moment. Then Thordis' body diminished back to its normal form. The bear raised his huge paw and brought it down upon the young man, slashing his chest.

Thordis collapsed and went unconscious. When he came to, the bear was gone. Thordis reached beneath his garments to touch his naked chest. The slash was there, yet already healed and scarred as five distinct lines scripted into his flesh.

When dawn filled the sky, the sage arrived at the foot of the mountain to bring Thordis back. They entered the ceremonial stone hut together and the old man began to chant. After many minutes of song, the sage lit his pipe and through the curling smoke he uttered, "You no longer need the ring. Its enchantment is within you."

From that day forward, the sage began to teach Thordis. He gave him all the instructions and instruments of the healer. All the songs and lore, all the old methods and remedies. And, before he died, he handed Thordis a bundle of tinctures and herbs and stones and bones that had been handed to him many decades earlier. And Thordis served his people faithfully until his own death many, many years later.

On that day, his own sons adorned Thordis' body simply and lay it in a small wooden boat. They set the boat afire and pushed it out to sea, as was the village way. As the boat floated out in flames, they sang Thordis' soul home to join his father and mother and many more ancestors who even now sit ringed together somewhere between the sky and the water, smoking pipes and trading stories much like this one.

THE KING AND THE DEER MAIDEN

Once there was a faraway kingdom held in kind leadership by a charismatic king and queen who enjoyed riches of various sorts. The people of their castle and surrounding kingdom were compassionate and generally content. Their hunts were often successful and their crops quite productive. Fine wine and ale were made and kept in plenty. And the most expert jesters, minstrels, musicians, dancers, and poets frequented the court. They had mighty horses and kept good relations with neighboring kingdoms, other than an occasional skirmish. Life was close to perfect.

Now, the queen, in addition to being regarded as very fair of face and extremely sharp of wit, was renowned for her skill in dance. To watch her move was to be mesmerized. It was her dancing, in fact, that first seized the king's heart and led him to woo her.

Well, it came about one spring that a young maiden from an unknown land arrived at the castle gates. She had traveled many months in the hopes of studying dance with the queen. Her presence was breathtaking. Her skin glistened, her hair shone, her smile radiated. She was dressed simply, yet elegantly, and a soft deer tail dangled from her waist belt.

She was well received by the queen who held dance sessions with younger women, passing along the intricacies of the art she knew so well. The maiden excelled and advanced quickly in the group and was much adored by the women of the kingdom. After some time, they seemed to think of her not as an outsider but as one of their own people.

The king was always busy with matters of the nation, in meetings with his council, voyaging to meet with other leaders, and hunting when time permitted. One evening, after a long day in council, he wearily descended the staircase to sit beside the fireplace. The maiden, who kept a room on the castle's ground floor, was passing through on her way to the kitchen. As she politely bowed and moved along, the king found himself smitten. The maiden's visage and form fastened in his mind and, from that point on, frequently resurfaced in his imagination.

Three days hence, the maiden was brought by the queen's request to dance at the royal dinner hall. Her movements were smooth as water, her limbs lithe and nimble. More than that, her face exuded a passion that intrigued the king beyond his will. She was so alike the young queen he had wed decades earlier.

The following day, the king saw the maiden ride out of the palace yards on horseback, her dark hair streaming behind her. She caught his eye and grinned as she galloped away. The king, though he dearly loved his queen, felt himself longing to be that gallant horse with the maiden's legs wrapped around him, her breath heavy and skin perspiring in the stride through fields and forests. A fire lit in his belly; he was undeniably enchanted past any semblance of reason.

That evening, the king walked near the maiden's chambers and came upon her in a dim-lit stretch of hallway. She smiled and bowed shyly yet she felt his manly instincts aflame. The king presented his hands to the maiden and she delicately laid her palms upon his. He softly kissed her hands and whispered, "I'm glad you're here with us."

"As am I, your lordship," she replied. And slipped away.

Three days later, the king found the maiden sitting in the study. He stood beaming before her. She rose to greet him. He approached and reached out to lightly touch her cheek. "Is there anything you desire?" his mellifluous voice beckoned.

"Not at all, your grace. I am quite satisfied." Her eyes betrayed her words and scintillated in the low light. She fingered the deer tail at her waist and gazed deeply back at the king.

The next day, the king summoned the maiden to his throne room to dance for him once again. He called no musicians to accompany her. The two were alone. She danced as she had never done before, leaping and spinning, and wildly circling her hips and whipping her long hair about. As she quieted her movements, the king exploded into applause and rose to embrace her. When he did, his longing filled his breast and he pulled her closer. The maiden sank into his hold for just an instant, then sprang back.

"Forgive me, your grace. I must away," she drew her hands to her face and scurried out.

In the days and weeks that followed, the king began to neglect his body. He ate little and slept poorly. He also neglected the kingdom's lands, their crops and hunts, their political relations and financial commitments. None of it held his attention as before. The king and the kingdom soon weakened. Little meat came in from the hunting parties. Some fields were left untended and did not produce. Two disputes rose with kingdoms where peace had been long-standing. It was a dire situation.

The queen approached her husband one evening in their private chambers. "You are a shadow of the man I knew. You've become bewitched by my maiden girl. Go to her and find your bliss," she breathed and left him to slumber alone.

The next dawn, the king opened his window to again find the maiden on horseback. He quickly pulled on his riding pants, grabbed his cap and flew down to the stables. In moments, he was in pursuit of her. He caught her horse's tracks and followed them into the wood west of the castle. Deeper and deeper into the forest, they rode. The king was speedy and came close enough to see the maiden pass between two giant ash trees. On the other side, the horse and lady were no more. A marvelous doe bounded along in their stead. Astonished, the king rode harder now, resolved to overtake this creature and discover its secrets.

The doe fled with all its might, racing up and down hillside after hillside, tucking into narrow culverts and gulleys, on and on, going beyond all territory known to the king. Yet he followed this magicked being for a great distance until his horse fell to the earth in exhaustion. And then the king continued on foot. The deer slowed enough for the king to stay apace with her. Yet she never stopped, leading the king on for many more miles until he too collapsed. His body had given out, he could not rise.

The deer pranced up to him. He saw the maiden's eyes shining in the animal head. A voice, from dream or delirium, sounded in the king's ears, "*Give over your most precious possession and you will be released.*"

The king took pause. The moment stretched out widely around him. He reached underneath his cloak to an inner pocket where an old hazel wand was wound in securely. He unfastened its ties and clasped the smoothed hazel stick. It fit his hand to perfection. The wand had been cut and carved by an old sorcerer a century ago. It was gifted to him at his grandfather's death bed.

The wand had come on every ride, every outing, every hunt, every battle. He held it in the council meetings and in his public declarations. Only now, crumpled and defeated by this otherworldly deer maiden, would he consider giving it over. He felt death looming above him and knew there was no choice. He must break this spell.

He laid the wand upon the earth and instantly felt a heat beside his breast where the wand had been. The warmth spread throughout his body. He felt restored, replenished, and invigorated. And cleansed. He rose to stand in the grasses that even now were greening and thickening around him. The deer blinked at him knowingly and bounded off.

The king turned toward home. The way was made straight and easeful, the miles seemingly trimmed in the newfound grace that enfolded him. He strode into the palace grounds on foot and walked directly to his queen who stood outside the castle. He flashed his legendary smile, and she knew he was back. To the king's refreshed eyes, the queen appeared imbued with an unsurpassable beauty, and he was more taken with her than ever.

In the weeks ahead, the queen found inspiration and returned increasingly to her dancing. The king would often watch and was mesmerized by her command of movement. Her sequences made time stop and charmed him in a way he had not known previously. The two enjoyed a deeply satisfying love. And the kingdom again flourished. Wealth of all kinds flowed in and was shared generously.

One day, a new sorcerer arrived, sent by a fellow king who knew his compatriot was in need of someone to hold that trusted role. The king put the sorcerer through a series of tests and found him to be true. The sorcerer was then charged to craft and properly enchant a new wand that the king held thereafter. It often cured the king's ailments, helped him vision clearly and discern rightly, brought many deer and elk to the royal table.

And the king discovered a newfound sense of himself and the world around him. Each day it seemed he was more in tune with his people, his lands, the way of things. Often, he sensed things about to occur just before they did. Even more often, he felt ushered through life, as if he were in a river and its currents moved his hand and mind more than his own will. And when he stood to speak, before the council or above the courtyard to the entire kingdom, the words came easily.

Peace was the rule of the kingdom and of his heart for a goodly number of years until the day the king lost track of his footing and came tumbling down the main castle staircase and landed in a heap at the bottom step. He never quite found his step again and retired to his chambers where he prepared himself for death.

The end came quickly and gracefully. The king stopped his meals and eventually took in no fluids either. He asked the sorcerer to chant for his soul. For three nights, the tones continued and for three days the king was visited by his children, his council men, and especially his queen. And then he simply uttered, "It's time. I'm going home," and breathed his last. It is said a track of extra brightened stars was visible that night from the horizon up to the zenith and all were sure the stars marked the king's path up into the heavens.

THE STRANGER

In a fertile coastal valley, a great ancient city once rose into being. Its makers were very intelligent and skillful. They contoured their lands and engineered their waterways. They cultivated all manner of crops. They husbanded robust animals to labor on their behalf. They built magnificent dwellings for themselves and marvelous temples for their deities. Over the centuries, it became more and more rare to find a wild, unmanicured place anywhere in the region. In fact, this city was more advanced and maintained than those of today.

To one family, a girl was born who, as she grew, became increasingly malcontent. Though she was among the most privileged caste and though she was lovely and smart and well-liked, she was unhappy and felt alone in her distress. She couldn't name it or even quite describe it, but she was sure that a poison ran through the city, underground and unseen, yet infiltrating everyone and everything. She even sensed that others were aware of the poison yet kept quiet for fear of retribution. So, when she came of age, the young girl left the city and ventured out on her own. To nowhere in particular. For few people spoke of life outside the city and she knew only that she must go find what else was in the world.

She traveled far, even sailed across the ocean, until she came to a village high in the mountains where a little known and little regarded people had lived for a very long time. Although their eyes and skin and hair were not like hers, they welcomed her. She quickly learned to cook and sew and tend plants. And she was especially loved by the children who raced around and played games with her and who were mesmerized by her strange language that sounded to them at times like a squawking crow and at other times like a hissing snake.

But, among the adults, she often stayed in silence. Listening. Learning. Within months, she was fluent in their tongue. Still she rarely spoke, preferring to absorb the tones of the words and the rhythm of the conversations held by this people so unlike her kin. Because she preferred to forget her old life and so refused to tell her name, the people simply called the girl Hu'moon, which simply means Stranger, for they had never seen anyone of her kind and were indeed fascinated by her. And came to dearly love her.

Something completely new to Hu'moon was how the lives of these mountain people were guided by rituals. When they planted or harvested, awoke or bedded down, gave thanks or encountered grief, the people were always speaking aloud to invisible beings who seemed to be ever-present. And who apparently loved when a fire was lit for them. Or an ornamental bowl was laid out in their honor and filled with spring water. The mountain people had special rituals at certain times of year. At these, the most beautiful songs were chanted by the lead singers. And the most spellbinding tales were spoken by the head orators. At the end of those celebrations, an old person could always be found sitting beside the glowing coals. It was said that whatever the people needed to know could be seen in the coals on those particular days.

It happened, some years later, that late at night after the summer solstice ritual, an old woman sat by the coals and saw that Hu'moon would leave their village. She gently called Hu'moon to her, and they spoke at great length. Although Hu'moon was afraid and knew not where to go, she had already felt the call yet had been unsure how to tell anyone about it. The old woman assured Hu'moon that she was ready for this change, that she had learned enough from the mountain people. And that the coals showed a long and fruitful life ahead.

So Hu'moon set out. Down the mountains and across the wide plains to a forested land that held a small village. This somehow felt to be the right place to stop. She was offered a hut at the edge of the village and stayed there alone, living simply and quietly. After a time, a gentle and handsome man came to her hut holding a string of rabbits in one hand and a line of trout in the other. Hu'moon was comforted by the man's kind eyes that softly reflected the light and she made a place for him at her table. Their bond of love was instant and it was not long before Hu'moon was growing large with child. The first was born and followed by another and another and another.

Their life was very sweet until the day the second child fell ill. His fevers raged more each night and Hu'moon feared for her son's life. It was then she remembered her time with the mountain people. That night, she dreamed of the old woman who had sat with her by the coals. And soon it seemed she was dreaming with her rather than of her. The old woman showed Hu'moon what to do for her son.

She awoke in the darkness and lit a fire and gathered water from the stream. By the fire's light, she filled a gourd with seeds and made her first rattle. And began to sing. All the songs she had heard in the mountains were present in her; they rose from her belly and sounded on her breath as naturally as a baby's cooings. She sang and sang. Her man woke and crawled over to the fire. He lifted two stout sticks from the soil and clapped them in time to the chants. It wasn't long before their son's eyes flickered open. And soon after, he was sitting up. Hu'moon took a coal from the fire and incensed her son with the smoke of mountain herbs. And she lifted a clay cup of the stream water to his mouth. And slowly, the boy returned to himself. To the earth. From some faraway place that had nearly claimed him.

Hu'moon was incredibly thankful. So much so that she lit a small fire and gathered a bowl of water each morning for many months until this became part of her daily routine. In the trance of flame reflected on water, many new chants came to her. And many tales. Indeed, her reality seemed to take on the shape of the songs and the character of the tales. Her upbringing in the great city seemed like a distant, fading memory. Eventually others heard about this strange woman and her fires. And they arrived. Perhaps curious. Perhaps desirous. Following an instinct that Hu'moon knew or carried something they needed. Or wanted.

Hu'moon received all guests with grace and honor. She made a spot for them by her fire. She shared with them from the stores of her man's hunts and of their gardens. And she freely offered them her songs and tales. Many came to see her. Each visitor seemed revived by the fire and cleared by the water. They felt so good when they left that they told others about it. More and more people came each season. The circle by the fire became large. And people's recounting of what happened there often expanded past the truth. After a time, Hu'moon was more her reputation than herself. People who came now expected healing from ailments, clarity of quandaries, a fix to whatever was broken in them.

The people who came were often deeply troubled. Hu'moon remembered her girlhood surrounded by the city's invisible poison. Now many insidious poisons were in her midst, visible to her in the eyes of each person circled around her. It was overwhelming. Once again, Hu'moon dreamed with the old woman. The dream showed multitudes of people retching on the earth and her own small family engulfed and swept away in the foul-colored torrent. The next day, Hu'moon snuffed her fire, wrapped up her water bowl, and closed her hut to all visitors. People were furious. Outraged. They demanded retribution. They claimed Hu'moon had promised them healing and could not abandon them partway through the process. Things were in turmoil.

Hu'moon and her family kept to themselves until one day, word came that Hu'moon's father had left his body. And that her mother was devastated. She gathered her essentials and traveled with her man and children back across the ocean and along the winding roads to her birthplace. She was astonished at what she found there. The once gleaming, prosperous city was in shambles. The forests were bare and lifeless. The waters were murky and stinking. The fields were dry and empty, and the animals were sparse and spindly. It was as if the poison long hidden had risen and overtaken the city. As well as her father's life. Hu'moon spent several months with her mother until her children became restless, and the family returned home.

After the arduous journey across land and sea, Hu'moon and her family arrived at their small village. It too felt changed. They immediately knew they would not return to their former hut and instinctively trekked up into the mountains, leaving everything behind. In the mountains, they began to build a new home from the stone and timber of the forests. They hunted small animals, ate wild plants and roots, drank from the stream, and worked. They built and farmed and crafted.

And, after several turns of the seasons, Hu'moon again made a small circle of stones, collected some sticks, and lit a fire. She unwrapped her special bowl, filled a jug at the stream and poured the water. She sat. And she sang. And her man and their sons and daughters came and sang, too. And told stories. And laughed. And did so morning after morning, night after night. And felt content.

And, after a time, people came to visit them. They were welcomed. They were fed. And gifted. Some seeds from their farm, a trinket from whatever they were crafting, something special from their shelves. Hu'moon always knew what to give the person standing before her. A small bone, a shiny stone, a medicinal plant. And always a song. Or a story. Sometimes a tiny snippet of a chant or the briefest anecdote would suffice. And the visitors left satisfied. And newly oriented. To find their own way again.

Hu'moon and her man lived that way until their children were grown and left the mountains. And they continued to live that way long into their elder years. Visitors became less frequent, but their stays were always memorable. It is said that Hu'moon's skin began to resemble tree bark. That her hair was indistinguishable from moss on a boulder. That her eyes became sharply bright and animal-like. That her toes lengthened and curled into the soil. Some even say a faint layer of feathers sprouted along her neckline. Still others swear they glimpsed the nubs of wings risen on her shoulder blades. Most strange of all are the reports that sometimes, when she spoke, her voice blurred from words to washes of sound that could not be separated from the stream's bubbling rush. And when she sang, that certain notes lifted beyond human register into screeches as sharp as any raptor song.

And legend has it that one day a visitor came by and found the log and stone houses empty yet impeccably cleaned. And found a small scroll upon the table. The opening words inked upon the parchment were, "Welcome home. If you choose to remain here, you will lead a beautiful life. But also one rife with complexity, and sometimes danger. You will not be released from this place until your death, but while here, secrets and mysteries beyond explanation will be visited upon you."

And that man knew he had found what he had long sought. And lived his life there. As did another after him. And another. And so on. And there is very likely someone there now, sitting beside the blazing fire or along the mountain stream. Alone perhaps. But rarely lonely. And alive in a way that most humans never know.

ACKNOWLEDGMENTS

My gratitude overflows to:

My beloved partner, Julie Madi, whose matchless ear is always the first to receive my poems and whose magnanimous heart ever steadies me.

My radiant children, Anjamora Ishi, Tadhg Iolar, and Fiadh Rimse, who are cherished above all else.

My mother, Chris, and my late father, John, who have lovingly supported me at every moment, including the choice to be poet and not priest.

My mother by marriage, Patricia Riggan, whose ongoing prayer and care has helped clarify my path.

My brilliant maternal mentors, Briana Rose and Louisa Putnam, whose words and presence have been guiding lights.

My dear friend, David Abram, who takes occasional nourishment from my spoken poetry and thereby feeds me a hundredfold.

My Green Man brothers who offer me a place of belonging and purpose.

All earth cultures that held poetry and myth at the center of their cosmology.

Timothy P. McLaughlin is a poet, celebrant, and co-founder of the Praising Earth Center for Arts & Nature. He has a longstanding devotion to weekly wanders in the wilderness where he finds his poems. His previous collections include *Rooted & Risen* and *Seeds Under the Tongue*. At Praising Earth, McLaughlin facilitates the *Green Man* programs, guiding men into a deepened conversation with life through the languages of poetry and myth. He lives with his wife and children in the mountainous Rio en Medio valley of northern New Mexico.

TimothyPMcLaughlin.com

Thunderous Press & Studios publishes writings and music that celebrate nature and produces live performances of music, spoken word, theater, and dance.

Thunderous is a subsidiary of Praising Earth, an organization that works to enliven humanity's relationship with nature through the creative arts and land stewardship.

PraisingEarth.org

www.ingramcontent.com/pod-product-compliance
Lightning Source LLC
Chambersburg PA
CBHW020544030426
42337CB00013B/968